D1456503

Sentimental
ECONOMY

Edoardo Nesi

Translated from the Italian by Antony Shugaar

OTHER PRESS

New York

Production editor: Yvonne E. Cárdenas
Text designer: Jennifer Daddio / Bookmark Design & Media Inc.
This book was set in Kepler and Trade Gothic Next
by Alpha Design & Composition of Pittsfield, NH

1 3 5 7 9 10 8 6 4 2

Library of Congress Cataloging-in-Publication Data
Names: Nesi, Edoardo, 1964- author.
Title: Sentimental economy / Edoardo Nesi ; translated by Antony
Shugaar.
Other titles: Economia sentimentale. English
Description: New York : Other Press, [2022]
Identifiers: LCCN 2021061172 (print) | LCCN 2021061173 (ebook) |
ISBN 9781635422146 (hardcover) | ISBN 9781635422153 (ebook)
Subjects: LCSH: Nesi, Edoardo, 1964- | COVID-19 Pandemic, 2020—
Economic aspects—Italy. | COVID-19 Pandemic, 2020—Social
aspects—Italy. | Economics—Sociological aspects.
Classification: LCC HC305 .N3813 2022 (print) | LCC HC305 (ebook) |
DDC 330.945—dc23/eng/20220107
LC record available at https://lccn.loc.gov/2021061172
LC ebook record available at https://lccn.loc.gov/2021061173

FOR MY FATHER

Where have you gone, Joe DiMaggio?

SIMON & GARFUNKEL

There was an endless future.

CARMINE SCHIAVO

Well Before the Pandemic

Some time back, well before the pandemic, the screenwriter and director Giovanni Veronesi, who had a show on TV called *Maledetti amici miei* (Damned friends of mine), reached out to ask me if I'd like to write "something about friendship," which would then be read on air by the actress Valeria Solarino.

I had only recently finished writing *La mia ombra è tua* (My shadow is yours), and I felt drained, but Giovanni and I have been friends since high school, and I didn't want to tell him no, so I tried writing it, this thing about friendship. Try as I might, though, it wouldn't take form, and just as I was about to tell him that I couldn't do it, it occurred to me that maybe, just maybe, I might be able to write something for my father, my babbo, disguising it as a message for a friend, because I couldn't stand to think about him anymore. I'd stopped dreaming about him, I couldn't even bring myself to cry about him.

I gave that a try, and it worked like a charm.

Anyone who knew me realized that I wasn't writing to a friend.

Those who love me understood and mercifully said nothing, and so, that evening—it was late, past midnight—I watched Valeria step on stage, lovely as the noon sun, and transmit my first message to my father since what had happened.

Oh, ciao, listen, I wanted to tell you something.

Yesterday I thought back to that interview with Muhammad Ali you read me a long time ago.

Where he says that Earnie Shavers hit him with such a powerful right it shook his kinfolk back in Africa.

It was such a hard punch that Ali's legs folded beneath him, and he was forced to cling to the ropes to keep from falling. Muhammad Ali, the greatest, explained that if he had been knocked to the canvas, he'd never have had the strength to get back up.

So he stayed up, wasn't knocked to the canvas, and somehow managed to survive to the end of that round and indeed went on to win the fight.

So, I thought maybe you read it to me because you wanted me to be like him in my life. Like Muhammad Ali. That you wanted me to refuse to hit the canvas, no matter how hard I might get punched.

But he was Muhammad Ali, and I'm just me. And I hit the canvas hard that day. And I stayed down.

For months on end, I stayed down.

I'm only now starting to get back up on my feet.

That's what I wanted to tell you.

That I'm getting back on my feet, and that I miss you. I miss you so much. I'd give my right arm to be able to hug you once again. Just once, that would be enough. But I know it's not possible, so I send you my best wishes.

And when you see him—Muhammad Ali—please tell him that I miss him too.

Taking Another Step

And then the world goes crazy.

"Today we've decided to take another step," says Giuseppe Conte on TV. "The administration has decided to shut down all business and manufacturing operations nationwide, except for those that are strictly necessary, crucial, and indispensable to ensuring a reliable supply of essential goods and services."

The date is March 21, 2020, and the prime minister of the Italian Republic is once again addressing the nation live, this time alongside a woman who's signing his words for the hard of hearing.

"We've worked all afternoon with the trade unions and the manufacturers' and professional associations to draw up a detailed list setting forth the manufacturing sectors, categories of production, and public utility services, the ones that are most vital to the continued operation of the state in this phase of the emergency."

We've worked all afternoon.

"All supermarkets will continue to remain open, as well as all stores selling foodstuffs and other basic necessities. So let me point this out: we expect no restrictions on the days that supermarkets can remain open to the public. There is no reason for any runs on stores. There is no reason we should see long lines, which would be entirely unjustified at this time. Pharmacies and other retail outlets selling pharmaceutical goods will also remain open. Likewise, banking, postal, insurance, and financial services will continue to be provided. We will ensure all essential public services, such as transportation. We will of course further ensure all related ancillary services that are necessary for those permitted essential services."

That was Conte, the university professor from Puglia who taught law in Florence and was elevated from complete anonymity only to be parachuted, unbelievably, into the office of prime minister, summoned by the populists of the Five Star Movement to govern Italy, in a coalition with the racists of Matteo Salvini's Northern League.

"The People's Lawyer," as he announced that he wished to be called and thought of when he took office, Conte visited the White House and loudly stated that his administration was a change government, exactly like Trump's government. Trump, in return, thanked Conte and called him "my new friend," going so far as to endorse him in a tweet, though he misspelled his first name as "Giuseppi."

Conte, Giuseppe Conte, who just one year after that day in Washington spectacularly switched his alliance, becoming the prime minister of a new coalition government of a diametrically opposed persuasion. In this new administration, the Five Star Movement replaced the right-wing Northern League with the left-wing Italian Democratic Party.

"We will slow down the country's productive engine, but we will not stop it," he says, and then he continues, dressed as sharply as a dance hall Romeo, making a special effort to appear solemn and heartfelt: "The state is here."

I cradle my face in both hands, I slowly start shaking my head while muttering under my breath that it's unbelievable, but then I lurch upright from the sofa and stride outside to my garden, where I begin watering the already-damp soil around my camellia tree, even though it's pitch-dark. As I spray the base of the tree, I snarl to myself, because I know that the obscene closing of ranks between industry and labor I've just witnessed is an extreme, last-ditch effort to stem the rise of infections, seeing that every day brings nearly a thousand new deaths, and outside the main hospital in Bergamo army trucks are idling, ready to haul off loads of coffins—I know it, and I expected it, like everyone else had. Still, this announcement disturbs me much more than the other, actually more terrible, announcement with which, only a few days previous, the lawyer of the Italian people had ordered us all to remain at home, doors locked and windows shut, allowing us out only to tend to *documented work-related necessities, situations of urgent need, or issues involving our health.*

What will happen tomorrow?

What will all these people do when their work is shut down—for the moment, shut down indefinitely, by the way?

There are *millions* of them. Where will they get their income, if no income is being produced anywhere?

And what is the meaning, anyway, of those three terrifying adjectives that Conte has just uttered, if and when they are applied to labor, which in the opening words of the Italian Constitution is boldly declared to be the foundation of the republic? (That is to say, of course, if no one has changed those opening words, in the still of the night, without alerting the rest of us, in compliance with some new and stupid iconoclastic furor.)

Necessary.

Crucial.

Indispensable.

What types of work, after all, are now to be considered unnecessary, not crucial, and dispensable, if the work in question allows a people to survive?

What jobs can we dispense with and still hope not to derail, in the first place, the economy itself, and after that the very fabric of the state, civil coexistence, and society at large?

And come to think of it, who makes that decision, anyway, people *who worked on it for a whole afternoon*? Who are they and what have they done, their whole life long, so as to be ready and able to make such a scalding, immense decision that is clearly destined to dig a ditch—no, make that a yawning trench—between the Italians, dividing them on the basis of some presumed necessity of their occupations, rewarding some and condemning others?

I snarl, of course I snarl, because I clearly understand that the death knell is tolling for the larger manufacturing sector once again, and especially for textiles, my beloved textile industry, but also for business and trade in general, for shops, for all stores, for bookstores, cafés, restaurants, and hotels. They'll go the way of the museums and movie houses and theaters and discotheques and concert halls and stadiums and sports arenas that have already been shut down, and the churches, because you can't even go to Mass anymore, or for that matter to public parks, and you're not allowed to walk on beaches or hike in the mountains.

How do you go on living without the unnecessary and the noncrucial and the non-indispensable? Hadn't we always said that those were what made life worth living, ennobling our existence, the pillars of what makes Italian style what it is, the things we stamp MADE IN ITALY, the flowers in our nation's buttonhole, symbols of the wonderful history of the special communion between art and craft and artisanry and industry and culture and environment and food and wine and tourism, this story that we told to an enthralled world, a world that had believed it, decreeing Italy to be the land of style and fine taste, the best country you could ever hope to live in?

Ah, this must be the ache of the phantom limb, because it's hurting as if I still owned it, our old factory, instead of having sold it fifteen years ago; as if my father were still here, still alive, and tomorrow morning I was going to have to muster the courage to pick up the phone and call him to work out which of the two of us would be the one to go down and padlock the front gate of our woolen mill, the Lanificio T. O. Nesi & Figli, because things are never really entirely gone, not even when they're over and done with, and neither are people, not even when they're dead—and Faulkner was right when he said that the past is never dead, it's not even past.

Fabio, the Bernabei

It was nice, though, the quarantine, lovely, really, with my daughter back from London just in the nick of time—Angelica on the last Ryanair London–Pisa flight, a flight I'd always cursed for the sheer discomfort they made you travel in, but ever since it delivered my darling daughter back to me just when she was needed, a flight that I now adore and will always root for—and my wife Carlotta, who never stopped making ravioli, and since we live in a great big house in the middle of a forest we could all live in peace and quiet, each left to our own devices, to read and study and listen to music and make video calls, and basically the only time we saw each other was at lunch and dinner, and then we'd have a gelato and sit down together to watch the TV series about Michael Jordan.

In the mornings I'd write aimlessly; in the afternoons I'd go out into the forest to run myself ragged with murderous, pointless labors, like raking off from an escarpment the oak leaves that had piled up over the years and kept the laurustine shrubs and ferns and broom plants and hornbeams from sprouting, such a heavy mantle of leaves that not even the relentless Saint-John's-wort could spring up and spread, and as I worked I listened to Bowie's "Lady Stardust" on endless rotation, turned all the way up. That song constantly, and no other.

Every evening I'd uncork a big bottle of white wine—some evenings more than one—and tell myself I needed to stay calm and hang tough.

Maybe because there weren't many cases in Prato, I was never afraid of catching the virus. With no rational reason backing it up, I lived through the whole pandemic in the absolute certainty that, even if I were to catch Covid, I wouldn't even notice it, because I was bound to be one of the asymptomatic ones. So I almost always went out to do the grocery shopping, invulnerable me, but the relief of being out in the world lasted several minutes at most. All it took was the sight of streets empty of cars to strip me of that sense of relief, all it took were the endless lines of people socially distancing in front of the supermarkets, the sound of my footsteps in the terrible silence of the abandoned city. Ten short minutes, and I couldn't wait to get back home.

Every day that passed, I was surprised at how little I missed the freedom to do all those silly, overambitious things that from time to time I loved to do on a whim. But when I mentioned that to Carlotta, she replied, "What freedom are you talking about? You never go out!" because, truth be told, lately I'd been something of a homebody, only leaving the house in the morning to have breakfast at the Bar Perugia, the café that Salvatore runs. He knew my babbo, had come to bid him farewell at Misericordia funeral home, and when he was there, face-to-face with the coffin, he made a sort of brief, understated bow that I'll never forget.

And then, out of the blue, a dear friend of mine dies: Fabio Bernabei.

During a brief interregnum when the Covid rules had been ever so slightly watered down, Fabio had chosen to defy the police checkpoints and had driven to visit a friend at his factory—very close to where I live, by the way: less than a mile away, as the crow flies. They were talking about the idea of producing masks when his friend had to take a phone call and Fabio took advantage of the opportunity to step out onto the balcony to smoke a cigarette.

"The call might have lasted two minutes, at the very most," his friend tells me at the funeral, and when he calls Fabio's name and hears no answer, he steps out onto the balcony and sees him lying on the ground, motionless. Then and there, his first thought is that Fabio must have slipped, and so he rushes over to him and kneels down beside him to help him to his feet—because Fabio is overweight, seriously overweight, and riddled for years with various maladies that both prevent him from having an operation and keep him from doing the physical exercise that would have gotten him into shape for an operation, so he just can't seem to get any better—and the friend shakes him and calls his name again, but Fabio says nothing and isn't breathing and just lies there, motionless, flat on his back, dead as a doornail, with the cigarette still emitting a plume of smoke between his fingers.

We'd been friends for ages.

He was older than me by seven years, but he lived on Piazza del Collegio, where I went to school, and he was a regular at the café across the street from the school, as well as a regular pinball wizard, and when Rossetti and other friends and I decided to put on a little student production in the school auditorium, well there was Bernabei, watching the rehearsals. Since he already had whiskers, we looked around, ready to tell him that he couldn't be here, but we had a chat before he left and next thing you know, we'd become friends, and friends we remained for the next forty years, and it would be hard to imagine a more loyal, sincere, and good-hearted friend.

He was notorious in the city of Prato for the rather unique relationship he had with money, so much so that he was universally known as Count Mascetti, the character played by Ugo Tognazzi in *Amici miei* (*My Friends*, 1975), the penniless aristocrat who'd run through his own estate and his wife's money as well, and then went on his honeymoon accompanied by a brown bear on a leash. Those who knew Bernabei well, though, understood that he was more of a Mascetti than Mascetti himself. After all, even though he'd never been wealthy—in fact, had always been poor—Bernabei invariably squandered what little he occasionally managed to earn with the same passion and verve as the legendary count, and if he had anything in common with Mascetti, it was the refined sartorial elegance he unfailingly showed off every single day, in particular his ability to use bright colors in his attire without ever seeming garish—especially notable was his gift for mixing and matching those colors.

He was fond of eating well and drinking well, and he never missed a single one of our Thursday evening dinners. He was fond of women, and had been married twice, but he'd been unable to make either of those marriages last.

Numerous are the legends retailed about him, for the most part unsubstantiated and destined to remain exactly that: legends. Among the best known is this one: sometime in the eighties, a TG1 television news crew had apparently discovered the existence of Prato, and one morning they arrived in the center of the city to get some footage and do some interviews, but found no one in sight because back then, in the morning hours, the citizens of Prato were all at work. It wasn't until noon that they finally spotted one denizen of Prato: none other

than Bernabei, who'd just woken up and was drag-
ging himself down the Corso Mazzoni in search of
his first espresso of the day.

"You, sir, must be the only person in Prato who
doesn't work. Why is that?" they asked him.

And he replied, without batting an eyelash:
"Work? I don't have the time."

Not that Fabio had ever actually tried working,
but at a certain point he and work must have nevertheless concluded that they were mutually incom-
patible, and decided to part ways, remaining good
friends as before, but agreeing never to frequent
each other again.

To me, Bernabei was a symbol of the idea that it
was possible to live another life, that it wasn't really
all that necessary to struggle every day of your life
to produce and earn, and that freedom was the most
important thing of all, more important than pride,
infinitely more important than money. Of course,
you'd have to be put together the way he was.

His funeral, too, was different from other people's funerals. To spend as little as possible, his
brother had decided to have him buried without
a Mass or any ceremony, without even summoning a priest to say a prayer, and so the thirty or so

masked individuals who'd come to the cemetery and had scattered out among the cypress trees in observance of social distancing only to witness from afar the unloading of Fabio's coffin from the hearse and the prompt lowering of same into a hole in the ground thought exactly the same thing that a woman standing beside me must have thought, because she spoke up immediately after witnessing that disgrace: "No! Poor guy!"

Then a gravedigger climbed up onto a small steam shovel and began plunging the scoop bucket into that pile of soft, fresh soil and dropping it into the grave. My friends and I ventured closer and stood there watching the coffin being covered with dirt, until another gravedigger showed up carrying a wooden cross inscribed with his name, misspelled—FABIO ABERTO BERNABEI, instead of ALBERTO—jammed it into the ground, and left.

All done. The ceremony was over.

The shortest funeral I'd ever attended had just ended, and we were all standing there gazing in astonishment at that heap of dirt and the cross when I felt someone touch the collar of my jacket—I had decided to dress like Fabio for his funeral: light-colored trousers, an oversized dress shirt, untucked, a navy blue blazer, a pair of brown Ferragamo shoes, quite flashy and elaborate, that someone had given me as a gift but which I'd never had the nerve to wear before: I knew that Fabio would have appreciated them. Last of all, a brightly colored Carpini scarf that I'd tucked into my breast pocket in an awkward attempt to pay homage to my friend who had just left this life, alone and in silence, unexpectedly, of a heart attack, in the midst of a pandemic, somehow dodging the threat of a respiratory disease in spite of the tens of thousands of cigarettes he'd smoked, not even a mile away from my house as the crow flies, carried off by a sudden but all things considered merciful death. And when I turn around, I find myself face-to-face with Bernabei's brother, the very one who'd planned out the infamous details of that funeral, the short, stout man in his early seventies wearing a polo shirt and a sleeveless red jacket whom I'd overheard explaining to the first Signora Bernabei that he'd chosen not to summon a priest *so that he wouldn't waste people's time*, and I was just a scant second away from picking him up by the seat of his trousers and heaving him into the grave alongside Fabio. Anyway, he told me, "I just straightened up the collar of your jacket."

As Soon as the Quarantine Is Over

At the beginning of May, the quarantine ends and we're allowed to leave our homes without our self-certification: I saved two of those documents, and maybe I'll have them framed, as a souvenir of living through a time when I needed to carry with me a sort of signed justification that I could show to the police in case they stopped me and asked where I was going and why. While in one I wrote, "I'm going to Pisa airport to pick up my daughter Angelica," in the other one I may have gone a little overboard, but still it was all true, and clearly that day I must have been upset: "I'm going to the pharmacy to get life-saving pharmaceuticals for my ailing mother."

Shops and cafés and restaurants and museums and parks all reopen, and we recover the freedom to do more or less as we please, but only a very few, chiefly the younger folks, hurry to avail themselves of that freedom, staying out until late in the piazzas and streets, giddy with joy at once again being able to do the tender, terrible things that young people do, indifferent to the fears and scoldings of their elders, who never tire of warning them to continue to take care because, as the television obsessively and awkwardly repeats, "This isn't the time to lower our guard," as if we'd all become fencers or boxers.

Then I, too, start leaving the house. I go back to having breakfast at Bar Perugia, I go out to dinner at Angiolo Barni's restaurant, and my friends and I raise a toast to Bernabei. One time I even went as far as Forte dei Marmi to take a look at the beach and the sea and the empty sky with Genova and Roberto Santini.

But it's not like it used to be. It's not even remotely like it used to be, for anyone. So one especially empty, disconcerting afternoon I go to visit the Mage.

He greets me masked, because that's the way things go in these miserable days: from one precaution to another, from one fear to another, even greater fear, and no one hugs, no one shakes hands, not even we do, even though we've been friends since we were kids.

He shows me his warehouse, crowded with pallets piled high with bolts of fabric that he still can't ship to his customers.

"That ruby-red bouclé with the astrakhan facing goes to Fuchs & Schmitt, in Aschaffenburg," says the Mage, as Alberto Magelli is known. He smiles because he knows that Fuchs & Schmitt was a customer of mine, a thousand years ago, and that I had gone to pay calls on them more than once, in that charming and tidy little town that is frequently referred to, though who knows why, as the "Nice of Bavaria." "That camel hair broadcloth, on the other hand, goes to Japan…"

Broadcloth! It had been years since I'd last thought of that ancient fabric, so unfailingly elegant, which I've always loved for the way it has of being both soft and spare, but also compact, even shiny, thanks to its short and perfectly flat pile that you'd expect to get roughed up the first time you touch it, to the point of twisting into a bout of pilling, but it doesn't because the Mage has flattened his "drap," his broadcloth—and rightly so, necessarily so—that is to say, he's kept it wrapped around a roll, spinning, for two full days at the end of all the processing, somehow, who can say how (gravity must have something to do with it, or alchemy, or both), acquiring that stability of appearance that will allow the customer to wear the overcoat made of that broadcloth for years and years without it ever looking worn or threadbare.

He then points out patterned jacket fabrics, flannels, velours, and *a separable double-faced electric blue fabric that's destined for Belgium, for Scapa*, another former customer of mine, whom I also used to sell a separable double-faced fabric. It was a miniature wonder of compound weaving, made up of two fabrics held together in a stitched frame that could, if desired, be separated, so as to give it a freer, looser feel. (I know that "freer, looser feel" might sound like a vague way to describe the qualities of a fabric, but in the textiles industry, that's just the way we talk.)

He still makes exactly what we used to make, the Mage. He makes wool. Classic apparel. Overcoats. I'm surprised.

"What kind of a price do you get for this stuff?"

"Well, it depends. Anywhere from twelve to sixteen euros a meter."

"Really?" I ask in astonishment. "That much?"

"If they pay me," he jokes, and then he heads up the stairs, toward his office.

The offices are small, but tastefully, and recently, furnished—blond wood floors, bright walls, black-and-white photographs of textile-related subjects artistically out of focus, a row of vintage bowling pins set up at the end of the office hallway, large Apple monitors dominating every desk, a slogan written in flowing script with flourishes and curli-cues on the wall of the sample room, decreeing in English that if you do what you love, you'll never work a day in your life.

He showed me a promotional video that features him walking through these offices, discussing fab-rics with the women who work for him. At a certain point we see him framed, smiling broadly, in a wide close-up, in a navy blue jacket with a white open-necked shirt, saying things like: *It always touches me deeply to think about how this adventure in my life first came about and where I've arrived now.* And then: *I'm in love with the work I do.* And then, again: *The evenings I spend with my customers, when in the end you start talking about any old thing, things that have nothing to do with work, are the times I love best, because you open up, everyone says what they think, you relax, and you find yourself speaking the truth, letting out what you really feel inside.*

I'm captivated as I watch that perfect identification of life with work, something that, when I worked for the family company, I'd never been able to achieve.

For me, going to work meant ceasing to be one person and becoming another: starting to think differently, talk differently, behave differently, even dress differently. Sometimes, while I was in the car on my short drive between home and office, it seemed as if I could feel it physically, that transformation, like the Incredible Hulk.

But for the Mage, work is life, and his company, La Torre, is a self-portrait. Since his father hadn't been in the business, he'd started at the bottom, so much so that the first thing he was told to do, on his first day working as an apprentice technician, was to paint his own office. After that, over time, with hard work, commitment, and passion, he became a full-fledged technician, and in time head technician and then sales executive. He came to the conclusion that it was a good idea to invest every ounce of energy and enthusiasm he could muster in the textile industry, focusing on design and production done in Italy. He was confident he'd be successful.

And so, in 2003, just a year before I sold my company, as I sat fearfully awaiting the impending Armageddon of my woolen mill and of the Italian textiles industry at large, the Mage went to his boss and purchased 20 percent of the stock of the woolen mill where he worked, signing a further commitment to take over the rest of the company at a later date.

His approach to the textile business is a clever one, capable of taking inspiration from the great fabrics of the past, but without slavishly copying them, because this is no longer the time for that mediumistic, visionary concept of fashion as the spirit of beauty that descends from the sky, embodying itself in a fabric, à la Sergio Vari. What the Mage espoused instead was an intelligent and deeply commercial textile industry, stripped of the patina of nostalgia, devoid of ambition and manufacturing challenges, delivered on time and at a reasonable price, perfect for these times of ours, sloppy and indifferent to the past. That approach allowed the Mage to sidestep his Chinese competition—"As far as I'm concerned," he told me, "they basically don't even exist, I buy nothing from them and I sell them next to nothing, 200,000 euros a year, at list price"—and over the years steadily build up La Torre's volume and revenue. Now, admittedly, La Torre is a very small company—there can't be even ten people working there, him included—but it's successful, because over the past five years, its turnover has never failed to grow, and this year, if it hadn't been for the pandemic, he might have reached a revenue of ten million euros.

He tells me that the pandemic devastated three seasons, not one.

"The winter season for this year, which was on the verge of delivering to customers, only to be called off. Summer, again for this year, which had just started showing samples, and was interrupted, and then summer for next year, because our customers have warehouses packed with items they haven't been able to sell and that they're certainly going to be pushing next year."

Problems started to appear as early as mid-February, he tells me. Foreign customers called him up to warn him that, since he was Italian, they could no longer agree to meet with him, and then came a hail of canceled orders and requests for extensions on terms of payment and for discounts.

"With the lockdown, revenue dropped to nothing at the exact same moment that costs reached their peak, when the orders had already been produced and our subcontractors were demanding payment, because we could hardly tell them what our customers had told us... They're all small operators, all Prato-born, and all great workers... I've known lots of them ever since school..."

"So what happened?"

"So I paid them, and I hope to be able to deliver all the bolts of cloth you saw down in the warehouse as soon as possible."

"And what now?"

"Now I'm experiencing a cash crunch, just like everyone else."

I ask him what the status is on the aid to companies that Prime Minister Conte has announced repeatedly on TV, that vast stack of billions of euros he made such a fanfare about on the evening news, and the Mage tells me that the money promised by the government still hasn't arrived.

"Maybe it'll be here by late June," he tells me. "But my company has a cash flow problem right now."

La Torre is a healthy company, but how could it have been ready to survive the challenge of more than a month's lockdown, only to open up and find itself in an industrial system that was by and large still shut down? Because even though his suppliers have reopened, a great many of his customers, and especially the retail outlets, are still locked down tight, all around the world.

"When they locked us down it was hard, Edoardo, brutally difficult...I sobbed like a baby, you know, I'm not ashamed to admit it...And I wept over tiny details too...I kept thinking back to when I padlocked the front gate of my company, with no idea of what the world would look like the next time I unlocked it...I even wondered *whether* I'd ever unlock it again..."

He takes a long pause, picks up a pen, turns it in his fingers, compresses his lips, then lets it drop onto the desk and turns away. I look down, focusing intently on the ornamental piece of glass that enjoys pride of place on his desk—a cornucopia filled with matchboxes from world-famous restaurants and clubs and hotels: Annabel's, Nobu, Brasserie Lipp, L'Avenue, San Lorenzo, Indochine, 7 Portes, Balthazar, Langosteria Café, Cipriani, Park Hyatt Tokyo, the Peninsula, the Standard.

"But now that I'm back in the office, I'm feeling more optimistic," he starts up again all of a sudden, and once more there's a smile on his face. "I feel certain that soon we'll go back there together, to all those places. You may think I'm crazy, but I have confidence. I export more than 90 percent of my production, my market is the world, and I can't imagine that Paris, London, New York, Barcelona, Shanghai, Tokyo, Milan, and Seoul aren't going to recover from this disaster and start to roll, like a cannonball, with all the people who are going to be even more excited about living their lives than before, and who are certainly going to want to go out and buy a jacket or a shirt or a suit…"

And he starts to tell me about the inexhaustible energy and excitement of the world capitals, the big cities he loves, cities that never sleep—the metropolises where things happen—the evergreen playing fields where people like him, not satisfied with how they came into the world, are constantly determined to get more out of life. As he talked it was as if his dreams took shape around us, and they are ancient and glittering, Magelli's dreams. They closely resemble the dreams my father had as a boy and young man, and indeed they are the exact same dreams. And the words, too, are the same.

"…and then just yesterday I saw a picture from France of an endless line of people waiting to be allowed into a Zara store that was just reopening, and I felt reassured. You know that Zara and Massimo Dutti are my most important customers, right? I told myself that, if that's the case, the world hasn't ended, and things are starting back up. Slowly, little by little, of course, and sooner or later we're going to get all this behind us, this pandemic, right? What do you think? How's it all going to end?"

I look at him and say nothing, because I don't know how to answer.

How's it all going to end?

I refrain from telling him that I don't like Zara one bit, because he already knows that, nor do I like people who buy their fast-fashion glad rags without a second thought about how they can sell them so cheap—except of course that they're obviously a product of the exploitation of the unfortunate sweatshop workers who stitch them together, on the far side of the globe.

I'm tired, very tired, and everything is weighing on me, including the thought that I'll soon have to return home along those same empty streets I took to get here—and the emptiest streets of them all are the ones in Chinatown, because the Chinese of Prato went into quarantine well before the rest of the city, and they observed that quarantine so scrupulously that very few of them must have caught the virus at all.

I don't even know anymore why I came to see him, the Mage, maybe I just wanted to come and drink from the trough of his optimism, and instead now here I am, faced with this immense question.

"So what do you think, Edoardo, will we get out of this in one piece, yes or no?

"I can't say," I tell him, and I get to my feet, "but I know someone who might be able to tell me. I'll ask him and then I'll come back and let you know what he thinks, okay?"

As the Sea Tosses

Every so often, when I'm at a loss in the face of events, I pick up the phone and call Enrico Giovannini.

It doesn't really make all that much sense to describe him by listing even a small portion of the many remarkable things he's done in his life, much less the positions he's held up till now. No matter how important they might be, they're always much less impressive than his intrinsic worth and merit, and I devoutly hope that the "celestial machinery" that the novelist Malcolm Lowry wrote about in *Under the Volcano* will turn in such a way as to ensure that Enrico soon becomes prime minister or president of Italy, so that he can finally steer the ship of state.

At least once—Italy can hope for such a stroke of luck, can't it?—it would be able to have at its head a deeply competent person who's respected around the world, someone who has unfailingly stood up for the more vulnerable members of society, a kind-hearted and honest person.

Enrico's not a politician. He's a world-renowned statistician and economist, and just to be perfectly clear, he's the diametric opposite of those overeager free-market fools who've been so relentlessly enthusiastic about globalizing anything and everything, while being incapable of glimpsing the distortions and disasters that ensue, even when they're taking place right before their eyes.

At the center of his work he's always placed the concepts of welfare and sustainable development, which he believes are inextricably bound up with social progress and are attainable through political means. Even in these cynical times, he has a vision and believes firmly in humanity and reason and science, and that is what I find most pleasing about him, more than anything else.

He's spent his whole life wondering about the signs that the present shows us, day in and day out, as harbingers of the future that awaits us—the same signs that politicians can't see or, if they do see them, seem to be determined to overlook, convinced that they're living in a never-ending present day that can be influenced with a tweet or two, deluded and complacent managers of the immediate now, stunningly similar in every way to those shipwreck survivors who paddle with their hands and fool themselves into believing that it is they who are moving the raft, not the tossing swells of the sea.

Well, Enrico Giovannini has spent his life studying the ways the sea has of moving, and I'm honored to be able to call him my friend, so now I call him up to pose Magelli's awful question.

He answers after just two rings, and behind his voice I can hear the silvery tones of his beloved nieces. I ask him if this is a convenient moment to talk about economics, and he hesitates for just an instant and then says yes, but I realize that he's busy and he's just trying to be nice. I get ready to say thanks and hang up, but then I decide that I can ask him at least one question.

"All right then, considering that during the lockdown the Italian economy was largely sidelined..." I begin, but he interrupts me immediately.

"I wouldn't say that. A substantial portion of the system has remained open, at least formally."

"Wait, what…"

"Go take a look at the ISTAT figures, they only came out a few days ago…"

He was the president of ISTAT, the Italian National Institute of Statistics, from 2009 to 2013.

"Wait, what do you mean 'open'?" I echo him in surprise, and I suddenly realize that I've once again fallen into the old illusion of identifying labor with industry, and industry with manufacturing, and manufacturing with small business.

I tell him that I'll go look at those numbers right away, but that once I've seen them, I'd like to talk them over with him a little, if he doesn't mind. He courteously makes an appointment to talk later that afternoon and thanks me, as if I hadn't disturbed him while he was playing with the girls. As we say goodbye, I think to myself how sorry I am that I'd never introduced him to my father, because I imagine they would have gotten along famously.

I go to check those numbers and I realize that Enrico Giovannini, naturally, is quite right.

A substantial portion of the system remained open.

The public sector—including the schools that moved online, as well as public housing—remained operational.

Post offices remained open.

Banks remained open.

Insurance companies remained open.

Financial entities remained open.

Agriculture remained operational.

Large-scale distribution remained operational.

Food production remained operational.

Pharmaceutical manufacturers remained operational.

The chemical industry remained operational.

The energy sector (including, of course, the oil business) remained operational.

Paper mills remained operational.

Transportation remained operational.

Logistics remained operational.

Amazon remained operational.

And all the ancillary industries associated with all these sectors remained operational, including maintenance and packaging.

The lawyers and accountants and notaries and architects and engineers also continued to work.

According to the text of the prime minister's May 22, 2020, executive order, moreover, we find provisions allowing the continuation of *fishing and aquaculture, the mining and drilling of coal and crude oil and natural gas*, the manufacture of *rubber articles* and *plastics*. What's more, the ongoing construction of machinery for all the industries that have remained operational, after which the text slips into vague terms, in part to avoid overlooking any given sector and in part to make everyone happy, and authorizes the continuation of the *repair and maintenance and installation of machinery and equipment*; *civil engineering*; *professional, scientific, and technical activities*; *the activities of executive corporate management and management consulting*; *news and communications services*; *the activities of economic organizations*; and *employment and professional activities*.

And the order allows wholesale trade in nearly everything, including *raw agricultural materials* and *live animals*.

The text allows the *activities of call centers* as well as the *activities of private security systems*.

Sadly, appallingly, the text states that the *manufacture of coffins* will also continue to be authorized.

It's a huge heap of things, and a huge mass of people still at work.

What about the pandemic?

In an ISTAT press release dated May 11, 2020, we read the other half of the story: the collapse of Italy's industrial production, which is described, a few lines farther down, as *an unprecedented plunge.*

The sectors that have suffered the worst are the *manufacture of motorized vehicles* (down 52.6 percent); *textile, apparel, leather, and accessory industries* (51.2 percent); and *metallurgy and the fabrication of metal products* (37.0 percent).

The trade figures are, if possible, even worse. In March, the general index collapsed by 30.1 percent, and in April, the plunge was a further 47.6 percent.

The revenue of hotels, bars, cafés, restaurants, and other public facilities dropped by 53.9 percent in March and 92.6 percent in April.

Transportation products and services—that is, the sale of motorcycles, automobiles, fuel, and airline tickets—lost 64.5 percent in March and 81.4 percent in April.

Apparel and footwear dropped by 56.5 percent in March and 88.9 percent in April.

These are disastrous numbers.

They tell the story of a ravaged economy, they demonstrate its extreme, unprecedented fragmentation, and put to rest once and for all the very idea that there can still be one common economic destiny for the whole nation, or that the aggregated statistical data of the nation's condition—the GDP, first and foremost—still hold anything like a minimal ability to describe its state of health.

Those who remained open and operational— *the industrial concerns deemed necessary, crucial, indispensable*—lost very little or actually gained, while for the companies that were shut down— frivolous and useless enterprises, evidently—and for nearly all trade, it was an unprecedented plunge.

The economic fates of Italians have once again been separated, then, and after the tsunami of globalization that swept away thousands and thousands of small businesses and shops at the turn of this new, misbegotten millennium, now it is the virus that has struck, laying waste to the same type of businesses and shops and the same exact people, with if anything a greater destructive force. It was as if entrepreneurial initiative, even the smallest and most trivial sort, had become an unforgivable defect in the twenty-first century, a scarlet letter— thus creating new and infinitely deeper differences in a social fabric already torn asunder by inequities and inequalities.

While for months we had been warned—by the television and the radio and the newspapers and the websites, by virologists and epidemiologists, by journalists, by television announcers, by politicians of all stripes, by actors, by singers, by soccer players and tennis champions and even Formula One racers—to stay home and wash our hands and wear a mask, in response to which we obediently stayed home and washed our hands and only went out to buy food and fill prescriptions for medicines and always wore a mask. While the hospitals filled up and the cities emptied out and stark terror placed its iron grip on Italy, a substantial portion of the economy, and the entire structure of the state, remained open and operational, as if the virus couldn't possibly infect those who worked there, and millions of women and men continued to go to their jobs every morning, in open defiance of fate and even of death. Certainly, they were terrified, and they went unwillingly, and always, I feel sure, with the knowledge that they'd been forced into it. Nevertheless, they also managed to dodge the tremendous economic blow that awaited many millions of other women and men who waited, shut up in their homes, for the evening news, despairing and living in the conviction that the world by now was teetering on the brink of the apocalypse.

I wonder what our rulers will tell these people, once the pandemic subsides and there has been time to think about that decision and understand its effects. Will they go on with the platitudes that they never seem to tire of uttering, including the one that *people's health comes first*? And then what if someone asks them why call centers and plumbers and manufacturers of packing materials were allowed to go on working, but woolen mills and retail stores weren't—then what will they say? That according to the calculations and considerations of that fateful afternoon, certain companies and several million Italians could be safely sacrificed, like children of some lesser god? Or that the health of some counted for less than the health of others?

A Bunker in New Zealand

So I pick up the phone and I call Enrico Giovannini and I start out by telling him right away that I'm not going to ask him anything about the pandemic, or about how it was treated in terms of public health.

"I choose to assume that the best possible effort was undertaken to stop the virus, and that the mistakes that have been made, and mistakes were certainly made, were due to the complexity of the challenge facing those called upon to govern us. I don't even want to entertain the thought that had those things been done differently, it might have been possible to avert the death of many of those people, and also of the doctors and nurses who gave their lives. Because it's easy to say someone's a hero, but they really were heroic…I don't want to think back again to the obsessive afternoon press conferences, with those frightened old men who sat at their tables and recited the ever-rising death counts and infection rates, or the lines of army trucks in Bergamo…I don't want to have any more doubts about the fact that in 2020 the quarantine was the only tool available—however medieval a tool it might have been—to fight the virus…"

I have to pause momentarily, waiting for the faint hyperventilation that's come over me to subside.

"And since I know nothing, personally, about epidemiology or virology, and after all, it strikes me that even those who do know about those fields didn't understand much, I'd prefer not to talk about the virus at all, you see…What I do hope is that the virus disappears and never comes back, or that we find a cure or a vaccine that will save us all. No, what I'd like is to ask you a few questions about the post-Covid economy, thus defying the words that come down to us from Guicciardini, the Renaissance historian: *De' futuri contingenti non v'è scienza* (About the unknowns of the future we cannot guess). Would that be all right?"

"We can give it a try…"

"So, do you believe that the lesson has been learned and that it will be possible to take measures on a global basis to keep a tragedy of this order from ever happening again? In other words, do you believe that in this era of political consensus measured out with an eyedropper by the minute and in a time of scarce resources and unbalanced budgets we can still spend money to ready ourselves against the threat of an invisible enemy that might very well never even attack us at all?"

That was hardly the most brilliant question in the history of the world, I realize that, but after a moment's hesitation, Enrico Giovannini replies in his calm, unruffled voice, telling me that certainly, that's possible, indeed, it's necessary to spend today in order to protect ourselves from future threats or accidents, known or unknown as they may be.

"But that's not enough, Edoardo. We can't just try to foresee the future, we must also guide our choices in the present day toward other possible, better futures. Here in Italy, we do that very rarely. We're accustomed to taking action only after the disaster. Italy's Civil Protection, our emergency management agency, was created to provide help in the wake of disasters, and it does that well, but Civil Protection and the other institutions established to prevent and mitigate disasters lack the necessary tools and resources. As a result, it becomes de facto impossible for them to prevent disasters from taking place. They can only offer aid and succor in the aftermath. The prevention of catastrophic events, and the preparation of the socioeconomic system for managing them so as to minimize the damage to individuals and property, is the responsibility of the state—indeed, of many states, because in an interconnected world like the one we live in, threats don't stop at the border. And disasters occur, even disasters with only the slightest likelihood of occurring, disasters that had never occurred before in all known history…"

"The notorious 'black swans.'"

"That's right, black swans. Because a low probability is not the same thing as zero probability, and if you study mathematics then you're accustomed to reasoning in terms of probability…Many economists place too much reliance on linear models, but there are also nonlinear events, singularities, and when they happen they always catch us unawares, unprepared, especially us Italians, because we haven't invested in prevention and preparation…"

As Giovannini goes on, I find myself facing the enormous problem of trying to take notes on what he's just said and at the same time listening to what he's saying, like some stenographer. Since I'm not inclined to ask him to repeat himself, I immediately realize that I'm certainly going to miss a few things. As if that weren't enough, his words are baffling, and my mind gallops to keep up.

I get distracted remembering how in our woolen mill we invested in a very different way, like everyone else in our line of work. Because we invested, certainly, but with an eye to getting that money back right away, in a very short cycle: money for looms, looms for production, production for billables, billables for profit, and with that profit we might just be able to buy more looms. A perfect, complete, self-sufficient, self-nourishing cycle. Which has now failed.

"...only when a country feels that it's a master of its own fate and its future," Giovannini is saying, "and when it has national pride and self-awareness. We Italians haven't always had these characteristics, especially not the awareness of who we were and where we were going...A little bit like that character of yours who one day receives a phone call from his accountant telling him that he's earned seven billion lire [more or less four million dollars], and he just sits there, mouth hanging open, because he never expected it. I've referenced that story frequently, to point out that for decades Italy had no control over what was happening to it, and in the meantime it just kept running, breathless…"

"But the country was running in the right direction, wasn't it? People were digging their way out of poverty, they were aspiring to live more prosperously…"

"Yes, of course, but it was a process of getting rich that sprang out of once-in-a-lifetime, unrepeatable conditions…It was neither conscious nor understood…It was as if the Italians had climbed onto a stagecoach that was being hauled at top speed by runaway horses, and they did nothing other than to cling to the side, without a thought for the horses pulling it, or the plains they were crossing…"

I can practically envision them in my mind's eye, those thousands of stagecoaches rattling across an immense plain at breakneck speed, and there I am amid the crowd, tossed back and forth, caked with dust, standing on the running board, face buffeted by the wind, a young man holding on for dear life, watching my father as he held the reins and the horses galloped faster and faster...

"Back in those years that you love so dearly, it wasn't just the future that we had no control over, it was the present, too...

"But it went great for decades, didn't it? The country developed, it modernized..."

"Sure it did, but then the plains grew rougher and the stagecoach started to slow down, lose parts. No one really knew how to fix it, because they'd climbed aboard a fast-moving stagecoach, and none of them were mechanics, just cowboys, and they thought they'd been steering the stagecoach, but really, no one had been steering it..."

I grow distracted once again. Could he be right? Then who was driving? The zeitgeist? What on earth might have been the response from the independent cloth makers of Prato if anyone tried to tell them that they'd never been responsible for their own success? If they'd been told that all the credit really went to the zeitgeist? Bellowed obscenities, belly laughs, and fists slammed down on their desks.

But Giovannini has already lunged ahead, galloping along as I struggle to keep up, scribbling notes, and I curse myself for not thinking to record the phone call, and now he's telling the story of the farmer who's faced with the choice between eating his seed corn today or planting it to harvest crops in the future. And then he moves on to the classical model of democracy, *which is governed by game theory, so that the citizens demand solutions to problems and the politicians offer platforms for those solutions, and then submit to the judgment of elections.* Now he explains to me how social media and big data have deformed that mechanism, replacing it with another, so that the politician *already knows* what the voter wants to hear, and that is what he tells him, that and only that, with a continuous stream of dozens and dozens of posts on Facebook and Twitter that are constructed specifically—in fact, targeted—for that voter, using the same system that ensures that the advertisements I see on the internet are aimed at me and other people like me. Then Giovannini moves on, telling me that the manipulative mechanism can be pushed even further, until it reaches the point where it is politics itself that creates a voter's preferences—*thus transforming them from exogenous to endogenous, until it is able to influence the very substance of democracy*—and then satisfies those preferences with an appropriately designed post.

"You create the problem so you can offer the solution. *Let's just help them where they live. The ports are closed. Immigrants steal jobs from Italians.*"

"Isn't there any way to escape these manipulations?" I ask him. "Are we really such imbeciles, the human species, that we always just do what we're told to do? Because when all is said and done, that's how it works, isn't it? We're told to buy something, and we buy it. We're told to fear some future event, and we fear it. We're told an untruth, and we believe it…"

"The only way to defend yourself against manipulation is to invest in education, in schools and in lifelong instruction."

"Are you saying that if someone has studied to some extent, they're less like to believe all the bullshit that's on the internet?"

"Well, let's say that you've phrased it in a fairly colorful fashion, Edoardo, but not entirely inaccurately…"

And then Giovannini starts up again, referencing the theory of long tails, the extraction of preferences, Condorcet's jury theorem, the results of

PISA tests, which are the achievement tests given to fifteen-year-olds around the world every three years. He recommends that I read Drew Westen's *The Political Brain*. He reminds me of the utilitarianism developed by Hobbes and Locke and Adam Smith, and the belief that the highest goal of life must be the greatest happiness (in material terms, primarily) for the greatest possible number of people, and therefore that the utility of the majority must always be preferred to the utility of the minority. But then he immediately pivots to the economist Vilfredo Pareto, who insisted that utilities couldn't be compared, and that the better solution—the Pareto efficiency—could be obtained when some are better off, of course, but no one is worse off. (I know that I'm summarizing in a deeply pedestrian manner, but I don't remember much from my high school philosophy classes.)

"Hold on," I interrupt him. "Hold on for just a second, or you'll lose me...I have another question. What should we expect from the immediate future of the economy? Because the pandemic will end, someday, or at least it will slow down, and it will be time to start over again, and when that happens, how will we do it?"

"We have to decide what kind of world we want to live in tomorrow, Edoardo. And we need to think ten years out, but also with a view to 2050. What you want to become is something you decide today. And then you have to act. Because the return from the pandemic may prove to be an extraordinary opportunity to change things, to start over again in a different way. But first we have to make up our minds what kind of future we want to live in…"

And suddenly I remember him in that photograph, standing next to Greta Thunberg, in the Italian senate, during a press conference about the future of the world's societies, as he holds the wireless microphone for her because the microphone on the table had stopped working, and she, sullen faced as usual, clearly states: *You're stealing our future, you've lied to us and given us false hopes.*

"Explain more clearly…"

"Well, let's say that there are three basic types of attitudes toward the future. The first is the refusal to see the change, a stubborn determination to keep the same views about the world and to continue exactly as we have done over the past forty years, with the neoliberal turbocapitalism that we know all too well, growth at any and all cost, with the mythology of financialization and the supremacy of the market, always, no matter what…Ignoring the warnings of scientists, expressing annoyance with this obsessive interest in environmentalism, exasperation with people talking about the risks of climate change, impatience whenever the rights of workers are mentioned, even if we're talking about countries where salaries amount to little more than a bowl of rice…In other words, people who say something along the lines of 'If you'll just let us work in peace without constantly sabotaging our efforts, we'll make sure the economy starts up again.'"

"I know them very well, these gentlemen."

"So you do. The second attitude, on the other hand, reflects the fears of the individual, the citizen who has convinced himself that the past was better than the present and that the future will be even worse, and the only sound approach is to find the best way to protect yourself from the tempests that are buffeting our current lifestyle. Building a bunker in New Zealand, the way certain Silicon Valley tycoons have done, and living in it, surrounded by everything and everyone you hold dearest, hoping to survive the Armageddon by burrowing down and hiding out, ignoring the rest of the world because it's become incomprehensible and unrecognizable, living in the blind adoration of a past you hope to restore."

"Trump style..."

"Well, he's certainly one of the people adopting that attitude and applying it to a whole nation. Hence, isolationism and 'retrotopia,' as the sociologist Zygmunt Bauman calls it. Walls to be built. Good guys on this side of the wall and bad guys on the other side of it, trying to besiege and climb over it. Fear as a political tool."

"What about the third attitude?"

"Well, the third one is the attitude of those who believe that progress can still exist, and with it the dream of a better future, a sustainable utopia, to quote the title of the book I published in 2018. We need to use science and compassion together, we need to knock down walls and find the courage to change everything. Including, especially, our lifestyle. The way we think and the way we live. Because the truth is that we have no choice, as a community: the alternative to sustainable development is unsustainable development. Don't you think?"

"Certainly," I reply.

I say it again and I fall silent.

Progress

I fell silent, because Giovannini uttered that magic word. But I'm not sure anymore that I even know whether such a thing as *progress* still exists, and if it does, where I'd find it, what form it would take, and what it means today—and most important of all, how someone would go about rooting for it, advocating and fighting for it.

Sometimes I get the impression that progress is off-limits to me. That at a certain point, someone, somewhere, established an exam that you have to pass to be able to call yourself a progressive, and that the exam in question can and must only proceed following a recantation, a ritual cleansing. One that works by evincing shame at the sheer fact of belonging to my generation, of being born when I was, or else the family I was born into, or the place where I was born; by turning my back on everything I've said and done over the past forty years, inasmuch as I've been the reckless father of an environmental and social catastrophe that I never did a thing to prevent—in fact, a catastrophe that I ultimately brought about with my own behavior. Behavior that I once thought implicated only an individual responsibility but that I now realize is viewed as the unequivocal mark of an incompetence that is laid not only at my own doorstep, but the doorstep of an entire generation that should understand and accept the harm that, collectively and individually, it did to the world it was so busy building.

It matters not at all that at the time I might have considered these actions of mine to be entirely fitting and just, because in fact—in the unquestionable judgment of a twenty-year-old of today—they most certainly were not. And you had better be behaving in an entirely fitting and just manner these days, or millions of censors go after you, attacking and insulting you freely.

But I have no recantations to make.

Sinatra-style, so to speak, I believed in what I believed in, however misguided it might seem now, in the present day, and I believed strongly and firmly in progress, ever since I was a boy, and I learned English from listening to Bob Dylan songs over and over. I still know the lyrics to "Hurricane" by heart.

I saw it all around me, everywhere, that progress, not just in the music or the books or the movies we watched or the clothing we wore, but in life itself, and I always embraced it, which meant I felt I'd been absolved of the unspeakable crime of being a coddled child of privilege, because every single day I watched in rapt admiration the wonderful spectacle of blue-collar workers rising from poverty thanks to the jobs that my father and people like him offered them.

But progress—the very idea and vision of it, the field in which it operates—never remains stationary, indeed, it changes continuously, and looking back, I can say that I'm now happy and consider myself lucky to have been on the side of the right, and to have felt that I was, for my entire youth and even beyond, right up to the turn of the new millennium, when everything changed and what was "right" appeared in its new and unexpected incarnation, that cruel and failed approach that sprang from the rush to globalization, declaring inevitable and even just—thereby legitimizing—the exploitation of tens of millions of factory workers in Asia and the corresponding economic decline of tens of millions more factory workers in Italy and Europe and America, and with them the fundamental, providential middle class that was, perhaps, the single greatest invention of the twentieth century, providential for the way that it held society together—even though it was castigated and mocked, day in and day out, because that middle class was never, never once, understood by the great and the good of literature and film. It served not only as a hub and center of gravity but also as a clearinghouse for the original and inborn iniquities, providing a safe and unassailable haven for those who were uninterested in becoming entrepreneurs, welcoming those who rose from the bottom and didn't want to perform menial labor, serving as a shock absorber for the terrible impact of life and earning a living, making existence incomparably easier and kinder than it is today.

And that's to say nothing of the bourgeoisie, which for years has seen its role and its confidence and its wealth crumbling away day by day, and now can't even remember that it had ever been the dominant class, reduced as it is to selling over that very same internet the brand-name bric-a-brac—handbags, suits and dresses, wallets—that it bought twenty years earlier.

The bourgeoisie that I considered myself honored to belong to. The one that the most-renowned novelists and filmmakers described as a mere receptacle for those afflicted with spiritual poverty—in short, society's worst members. And they did this without any realization of the fundamental importance of the role the bourgeoisie played in ensuring society's welfare as well as the relative prosperity of those same factory workers that the great novelists and filmmakers were so interested in standing up for. Without any realization of the ineffably crucial role of the modest ambitions and modest goals that those workers stretched out to attain on a daily basis—because all at once those ambitions and goals seemed possible, attainable. Without any realization of the ethical quality and, dare I say it, the inherent *morality* of whole lives spent scrimping and saving in order to afford the purchase of things and then boast about those things to friends, thus triggering new modest desires that proved attainable and deeply human, and so on and so forth and on and on in a cycle that was fervent and simple and rough-and-ready and yet, all the same, virtuous, an exceedingly virtuous circle—doubtless unrefined, but what popular, working-class thing isn't unrefined? That circle was also indispensable, not only in terms of creating the widespread prosperity that our sons and daughters have only heard tell of, as if it were some fabled Atlantis, or the Phoenix that rises from its own ashes (understandably they're sick and tired of the legend), but also to make possible the kind of economic growth that we now chase after desperately—to the point that we rejoice in glee at even the slightest decimal-point rise in GDP we manage to claw away, unwilling to admit or even understand that the kind of growth we once took for granted will never come back.

I'm the son and heir to a ruinous collapse, then, not the father of it.

I come out of the thunderous collapse of every last stick of certainty that had been handed down to me, first and foremost a collapse in the confidence that there would be a just reward at the end of the long road of hard work and commitment, and for the past twenty years I've had to stand by and watch in astonishment at the tumorlike growth of a senseless and corrupt economic and financial system where interest rates are below zero but no one has the courage to invest and build. A world where nobody seems to need workers who know how to create, but instead wants only slaves shackled to the assembly line. As a result, wealth, instead of spreading beneficently the way it did when I was young, is now concentrated in the hands of a very few assholes who run roughshod over the nightmare scenario of a planet-spanning marketplace served by immense and monstrous industrial subdivisions that remain, as we have recently had the opportunity to observe, as fragile as they are huge, laying their foundations as they do upon the backs of those at the bottom, systematically and criminally exploiting those in the lowest echelons. This marketplace is driven and fueled by an idiotic, brainless impulse to buy, an obsession that assails us relentlessly, because it's incessantly reinforced by the unopposable power of the advertising that obscenely invades our lives, oozing out of the cell phone that we never put down, all of us—pathetic suckers that we are— laying waste to and deleting any dreams of freedom and community that we might still cherish, dreams that were once based on the word "internet," polluting our hearts and minds even more irremediably than it does the planet as a whole.

That's who I am.

This defeat, this rage, this fate.

The Unknowns of the Future

"...a serious and difficult situation, of course...But if you ask me how things are ever going to go back to normal," Giovannini is saying as my mind turns back to the phone call underway, "I don't know what to tell you, because, naturally, your fellow Tuscan Guicciardini is quite right, *De' futuri contingenti non v'è scienza* (About the unknowns of the future we cannot guess)... Anyway, one thing we can say for sure: the shock will be asymmetrical, very asymmetrical..."

"Because of the closure of the companies that are neither necessary, crucial, nor indispensable..." I chime in.

"Yes, certainly, that, too…But you have to consider that during times of economic crisis, it's always durable goods—cars, just to offer an example—and semidurables, say, clothing, that lose the most market, because consumers focus on other economic issues, on basic survival…I don't know how much work they would have done, the companies that were shut down, even if they had been left open for business, and the same thing goes for the shops…And then if we want to talk about a shock to the system, we should consider that the workers in the industries and the services that have remained open and operational have been paid regularly. The public servants have been paid regularly. The employees of the companies that were ordered shut down were put on state unemployment, and they may have received less than their regular salaries, in some cases a great deal less, but they did receive something. And when their companies open back up, they'll go back to their old salaries."

"*If* they open back up…"

"*If* they open back up, of course…But I believe that a great many of them will open back up, wait and see…"

"So, is that why we never saw the uprisings everyone feared? Because money was still doled out to everyone who needed it? I remember that people were talking about mobs assaulting supermarkets, in the newspapers and on TV…"

"Listen, these are huge resources that have been allocated, and it's forbidden for companies to fire their employees…People have been suffering, no two ways about it, but they haven't been left out on the street, without a penny to their name, the way they have in America, and even freelancers have been helped, some of whom didn't really need that help…Plus you need to consider the whole sector of under-the-counter employment. The sheer vast expanse of the off-the-books workers. Tax evasion. And the secret bank accounts of the Italians, as a nation, the world's biggest savers…These are all factors that have already partly absorbed the shock, and will continue to absorb the shock of the impact to the system. Obviously, not for everyone, and it's no accident that we insisted—[the politician] Fabrizio Barca and I—to establish an emergency income, so that we could be sure to help the lowest of the low, those who really had no other resources available to them, those who were left entirely vulnerable by a lack of coverage by any social services. I'm not minimizing the gravity of the situation, of course, and I'm convinced that we're heading for a very, very difficult period, but the factors I've just briefly laid out for you are aspects that should be kept in mind."

"So what will happen to consumer spending?"

"That will depend very much on people's expectations. From the messages that are sent."

"It'll depend on political factors?"

"Yes, in part. Consumer spending is something that gets decided not only in terms of how someone's doing right now, but how someone foresees the future, and how that future is presented to them. If you believe that the future won't be any worse than it was before the shock of Covid, you're less upset about having to dip into your savings to ensure the same quality of life. Individual mindsets are important, personal expectations are important, I'll say it again, and there are many who don't feel safe starting to spend again right away, even once they've gone back to their previous jobs. Some forecasts tell us that in 2020 the GDP will drop by roughly 10 percent, but that families' disposable income will drop by only 1.5 percent, as a result of government relief. That means that a considerable portion of the drop in consumer spending, and therefore of the GDP, will have been caused by a rise in savings, not a lack of income. And then there will be funds from the European Union…"

"So there'll be money…"

"If you look at the system as a whole, yes."

"Well, so?"

"If I were going to risk making a prediction, I'd say that consumer spending is going to continue to drop—considerably, even, because the effect of loss of confidence and growing uncertainty will push a great many to save…"

"What about consumer businesses? What will happen there? Bookstores, shops, restaurants, cafés, movie theaters, hotels…All of the sectors that produce the goods and services I use the most and I like best have been shut down—because they're public facing, directed at people who break away from their computer screen and get out of the house to buy a book or a shirt or a record, who hop on their motorcycle and go out to dinner…People who travel, who go to the movies, who eat breakfast in a café. People who aren't willing to settle for just *seeing* things, but want to *do* things instead…What's going to become of all those people, huh?"

"Well, that depends on how the shock is perceived, Edoardo, whether it's temporary or permanent, and in its turn that depends on a great many other factors: for instance, whether there's a second wave of Covid infections or not, and how much talk there is about it, and in what terms, before it finally arrives. Whether the vaccine arrives, or really, *when*. Here, too, psychology becomes fundamental, and we'll only know whether behaviors have changed in structural terms once there is no longer any physical limitation on the pursuit of normal human activities. But keep in mind, in the past, after a war, there is a period of euphoria, just think of the Belle Époque..."

I tell him about the Mage and the fact that I'd promised to go back and provide him with the answer to his terrible question.

"I think your friend will come out of this all right," Giovannini replies. "If he's as good at what he does as you say he is, he'll find a way to satisfy his customers' needs. He'll dream up some new system for producing and selling, maybe in a sustainable fashion...I know that it's easier said than done, but after all, that's how it's always been, isn't it? You all, who produced fabrics for fashion, didn't you have to reinvent yourselves every season?"

I'm reminded of Sergio Vari, who climbed up onto the stage with me and Mario Desiati and Fabio Genovesi during a presentation at a literary festival in Puglia. In the end, instead of talking about our books, we wound up discussing him and the incredible life he's led. But then, when I asked him to tell the audience some of the stories he'd told me about the designers he'd sold incredible fabrics to for decades on end, and all the actors and rock stars he'd come to know, Sergio shot me that shy, cunning smile of his and said, "Edoardo, those are personal matters." And when Mario asked him to tell us what fashion was, in that case, he replied: "Fashion is over."

"Maybe a whole new generation of entrepreneurs will spring up," Giovannini goes on, "kinder and fairer to their employees and to the environment, capable of satisfying new forms of demand. That's where the government needs to weigh in to help accelerate the transformation, protecting the more vulnerable players, but also assisting the transition toward a new model of development, perhaps by obliging companies to account not only for their profits, but also the social and environmental impact of their manufacturing and sales. And by so doing, maybe we'll rediscover the entrepreneurial culture of our country and the Italian economists of the eighteenth century, who proposed a model based on the civil economy and shared resources, but who lost the battle to the Anglo-Saxon utilitarian economists, considered to be the fathers of capitalism..."

I'm Twenty-Two Years Old

I'm twenty-two years old, it's 1986, and I'm in my babbo's office. I'm telling him that I don't want to keep working for the company. I'm sick and tired of spinning mills and warps and wefts and refinishing and the technical office and the sales office and the accounting office.

"I just can't take it anymore," I've told him, "I'm going back to the university, I'm going to enroll in literature or political science, I'll get my degree, and then we'll see what's what. I don't know, maybe I'll go to Rome and make movies with Giovanni Veronesi..."

He shakes his head and just keeps saying: "No, no, what are you talking about, Rome, what are you talking about, the movies..."

Then we hear a knock at the door, we turn around, and two factory workers have already walked right into my babbo's office without waiting for an answer.

"You guys?" he asks out loud, and they reply: "We knocked, Alvarado. Didn't we have an appointment? Should we come back later?"

"Come on in, kids," my babbo says, and waves for them to take a seat, relieved at this interruption of our conversation.

The "kids" are my father's age—fifty-five, my age as I write this—and to me they look like old men. One of them is wearing a pair of greasy bib overalls and a sweatshirt with the sleeves cut off, featuring the name of a twisting shop in Vaiano; the other one is wearing a checkered short-sleeve shirt and a pair of dark blue trousers made of heavy canvas, likewise filthy and grease stained. Grim-faced, powerfully built, unkempt, they go straight over to him, treading the gleaming marble floor and shaking hands with him. Then they sit down on the two elegant leather Frau office chairs across from his desk.

I'm about to leave, but Babbo gestures for me to stay and so I stand there, next to the big window overlooking the factory yard, right in front of them.

He points to me and makes an introduction: *This is my boy, Edoardo*, and they just give me a brief nod of the head and an *It's a pleasure*.

"Alvarado, we're here because we're at the end of our rope," Bib Overalls says, then looks down at his shoes for a few seconds and continues: "There's no way to go on working at our usual rates. Everything's more expensive: our electric bills, labor costs... The other day a picker belt broke and all the threads and the teeth were severed, you can imagine, it was a ca-tastrophe... Then we had to buy a replacement de-livery van, and even buying it used, it's still a lot of money... It's not the fact that we're not making any money, Alvarado, we're used to that, it's that by now we're losing money by the bucketful, we can't go on like this..."

Then Bib Overalls suddenly seems to deflate, as if annihilated by the sheer narrative of his own overwhelming misfortunes, and he turns to look at Short-Sleeve Shirt, who hasn't budged an inch so far and is just sitting there, as if under some sort of spell, gazing at Babbo.

"You tell him too."

Short-Sleeve Shirt snaps out of it and starts talking in a voice that is at once hoarse and stentorian, a voice that seems to emerge more out of the depths of a ravaged soul than out of the tobacco-smoke-marinated throat of an exhausted man, and I'm deeply touched by the sound. As he speaks, the two of them appear to me as the personifications of the writer Giovanni Verga's fieldhands and their lives, devastated by poverty and mishaps, ruined by a cruel and unjust regimen of labor that consumes human bodies and souls.

"We just can't keep this up, Alvarado, believe me. We don't make enough to feed ourselves at the end of the day. We have expenses, for our families as well, and by now when I go home at night I'm ashamed to show my face to my wife. Our kids are starting to go to school, and we have to buy them books and uniforms and shoes, because their feet keep growing…What are we supposed to do? Because we need our kids to study, not wind up like me, a miserable, poverty-stricken wretch…"

He says nothing for a moment, then looks at Bib Overalls and says, "Alvarado, we're here to ask for a raise. We want ten."

My father nods, inhales deeply, then exhales slowly.

"Guys, I was expecting this."

There is this wonderful American expression that means you're looking at someone and they look good, in great shape, elegantly attired and groomed, and visibly happy. *You look like a million dollars*, the Americans say, and in fact Babbo looks splendid in his greige Armani suit—"greige" is a color popularized by Armani, a sublime mixture of gray and beige that illuminates with that hue anyone who wears it.

Handsome as the noonday sun, with a gleaming white shirt and a knit tie, again Armani, his hair brushed back but at the same time graying and gleaming, my babbo really did look like a million dollars, and he glances at them and tells them he understands, because it's hard out there for everyone, but he can't give them a raise, because there's just no work to be had.

"This year, when the Germans piss it's barely even a stream, just dribbling drops, guys, and what little we can get them to order is at cutthroat prices, we can't even make back our fixed costs on it. So how can I even think of giving you a raise, eh? You guys tell me."

Whereupon my indignation spills over. How dare he spew this nonsense! He had just come back from Bavaria with an armful of orders landed at full list price, without so much as a discount, and the markets were humming along beautifully, all of them, not just the German market, even the markets that were less significant for us, like the Austrian market, the French market, and the Belgian market, and if we had any kind of a problem as a company, it was just how to manage to produce all the fabrics that were being ordered, and when all that was said and done, we still couldn't even give a raise to these poor factory workers who were at the end of their rope?

I was about to weigh in and say something, but they were already comfortably exchanging stories of horrendous poverty and impending bankruptcy, and then suddenly they're saying goodbye, with the promise that Babbo would have a talk with his partner, and that then they'd *take a look at things together and see what could be done for them.*

I watch them file out in silence, without even nodding in my direction, and when I notice that there's a string of white wool trailing out of Bib Overalls' pocket, I'm deeply touched, and I lose my temper. As soon as the door shuts behind them, I launch into a furious diatribe.

Because as early as elementary school I'd been bombarded with a steady diet of stories about factory workers exploited by their thieving bosses, and during music lessons in middle school they had us sing "Bella Ciao," and the tutors who came to catch us up on various subjects after the school day in high school had copies of the leftist newspaper *Lotta Continua* poking out of the pockets of their corduroy jackets, carefully and consciously folded so the headline showed. Eventually I'd metabolized the idea that work really wasn't anything other than a constant process of exploitation of labor by the owner and the boss—and that, once again, I was the undeserving beneficiary of privileged and unjust advantages wrangled on my behalf by my father, and not by me. After all, I'd simply had the dumb luck to be born his son.

Not that I was a Communist—no, not that, I had certainly never been one of them—but even if at this point it was already 1986, I still couldn't get it out of my head that this state of affairs couldn't go on, and was about to be replaced by a better, more just, more humane way of doing things, worthy and compassionate, which would eliminate the hateful inequalities that our society was ridden with, restoring justice to the world, and it would therefore be up to us, no, make that up to *me*, to take the first step and start to redistribute the wealth that had been earned on the back of the factory workers.

So I tell him that it's not right to deny these poor workers' request for a raise: it's cruel and unworthy of him, and shortsighted, and downright immoral.

"Workers should be paid a living wage," I proclaim, and then I add, unbelievably for the atheist that I was then and remain today: "They should be paid their fair due, even the Church says so."

My babbo stares at me for a few seconds.

"Edoardo, you don't understand a goddamn thing, let me tell you. We're negotiating: there's no reason to get all worked up. It's a bargaining process, we're talking about money here…And another thing, those men aren't factory workers: they're artisans. Do you know the difference?"

I shake my head.

"They're not employees of ours, they're businessmen themselves, just like us, but on a smaller scale. And they're coming to see me with a request, but don't misunderstand the balance of power, they're the ones holding the knife by the handle, and we're looking at the business end of it. They know perfectly well that if they stop weaving for us, we won't be able to make deliveries of the promised bolts of fabric to our clients. They know I have no choice but to give them a raise, so they're asking for ten because they're hoping for five in the end. You know, once all the shouting is over. But if I don't at least try to negotiate, if I don't make them sweat a little, come June they'll be demanding another raise. You understand?"

Stubborn as a donkey, I answer back that all the same there's just too big a difference between us and them, and it strikes me as neither fair nor good form to take advantage of poor workers being pushed to their limits.

"I was ashamed to see you do it, Babbo, I mean it. It's not like you. It's not ethical. It's not moral."

"Good form? Ethical? *Moral?*"

My babbo stands up and leaves the office.

"Come with me."

He's smiling; he seems amused. We walk all the way through the plant, and every time he meets a worker he asks him if he's at the end of his rope, and the worker smiles and walks on. Then we come to the window overlooking the street below, and there they are, leaving the plant, Bib Overalls and Short-Sleeve Shirt.

"Just look, they parked a long way off, and they did it on purpose..."

We watch them walk away, a good hundred yards down the road, and then stop next to a pair of identical beige Mercedes 200Ds, practically brand-new. They stand there talking things over for a few more seconds, gesticulating, and even at this distance we can hear the deflagration of emphatic and imaginative strings of obscenities, and then they bid each other farewell and set off like a caravan, in single file.

Babbo starts laughing.

"Well, just look at that, they *already* have the Mercedes-Benzes that social justice demands."

A Convincing Dream

I hear Enrico Giovannini whisper to someone in the room that his call is almost finished, and I shake my head and look down at my sheet of questions. There's just one left, so I ask it again, like a child: "Well, now what? What's going to happen now?"

"I'd like to be optimistic. But that's providing that, when things start back up, they start back up on a different basis. There's climate change, which needs to be dealt with differently. It's not as if the virus killed it as a problem. Earlier, we were talking about the fact that European Union money is on its way. Well, if we spend that money to rebuild old manufacturing sectors the way they used to be, that will be a big mistake. If we use the money to make deep-seated changes in those manufacturing sectors, making them sustainable, and especially with a view to building new sectors, on the other hand...Let's say, for example, that we stop saying and thinking that green development is a cost and start calling it an opportunity, an extraordinary chance to start the economy up again..."

I can hear him getting a little worked up—in his own way, of course, with all the urbane restraint he possesses—as he begins listing patches he'd immediately apply to the economy and the larger world with all the calm urgency of a father, the head of a household, while I try in vain to keep up with him in my note-taking.

"It's important to invest in the quality of individual human beings...We need to invent new jobs, new forms of work that are designed to satisfy new needs...A transformation of the system, strengthening it, making it more resilient, greener...This crisis can also be an extraordinary opportunity, but we shouldn't waste it by trying to save everyone indiscriminately, even the tax evaders, even people who shifted their corporate headquarters to the Netherlands to pay lower taxes...The roles of the state and the markets should be reimagined, enhanced...The state should make itself felt, assume a leadership role, a faculty of guidance, now that capitalism has become fragile...Transitioning to a circular economy increases productivity, it doesn't reduce it...We have to pay much more to repair hydrogeological and seismic damage than it costs to prevent that damage, while prevention creates jobs, quality jobs, that among other things can't be offshored...We don't have to build new skyscrapers if we can use the same money to renovate and rebuild whole neighborhoods...What I mean to say, and I don't want to go on at length, is that if we lay the foundations for building a different way of looking at the world, and living in it, then we'll be doing the right thing. And in that case, everything really will be fine."

I sigh, and he must have overheard me, and his tone of voice changes. It becomes more heartfelt.

"Edoardo, a piece of history is gone now and won't be coming back. A system has disappeared. There's no time to waste worrying about it, unless that's time we spend learning from our past mistakes. What we need to do now is invest in the future. *In* young people. *For* young people. And that means we can't strip them of resources they need to pursue policies that we're interested in. We need to provide them with resources. Not bury them in debt. This is the time to be generous. And we need to see growth, definitely, strong growth, but it must be in the context of a sustainable form of development. We need to restore some form of justice among generations. There's a possibility of doing it, believe me. After all, as is always the case, it just takes the will to do it."

He pauses.

"A dream needs to be shown, that's clear, but then we have to turn that dream into reality. Around the world, progressives only win when they have a persuasive dream to talk about. Otherwise, the right-wingers win, perhaps because they claim to have the solutions to people's fears. Fears that as often as not they themselves have helped to create."

"Because the alternative is intolerable." I manage to get a word in.

"Yes, the alternative is intolerable. It's this, right here, what we're living in now."

And it's breaking our hearts, I'd like to say to him, but I don't say it. I want to keep that little flame of optimism that he's just bestowed on me flickering, close and dear.

"The interview is over," I announce instead, and suddenly tears well up in my eyes for some stupid reason buried deep inside me, a reason I have no wish to talk about. I thank him and I say goodbye, and then I wonder whether I am now and whether I ever will be up to the task, whether we'll all be up to the challenge of the immense revolution that this calm and balanced man is talking about.

I don't know whether I'm closer to understanding it and approving it unreservedly, or just plain fearing it. I don't know whether it's a future that I can take on, or perhaps I should say take up, as if instead of an idea it were a rifle, because if we have any hope of making this idea prevail, it's going to be necessary to fight.

I don't know anything, it suddenly dawns on me. In fact, there's just one thing I do know, and that's that if I had him here, in front of me, Enrico Giovannini, Covid or no Covid, I'd give him a hug.

The Doni Tondo

Spring tumbles forward into a gentle, unassuming summer, without the atrocious, muggy heat we were all expecting.

All through June we live through seemingly endless, gently caressing days, and as I read and reread Joan Didion's collections of magazine pieces from the sixties and seventies, *Slouching Towards Bethlehem* and *The White Album*, I'm once again impressed by how peerless her writing is, the way it manages to convey the hollow heartbreak, the sense of helplessness of living in a time of immense change, the chilly anguish of being unable to do anything but watch while everything goes to pieces around you, and even as I see from the television news that the pandemic is raging in New York, I find myself hoping that she's safely holed up in her Upper East Side apartment, and that she hasn't gone out for any reason at all, the finest writer alive in this world.

One day my wife Carlotta persuades me to leave home, and we go back to Florence. She wants to take me to the Uffizi, to see the *Doni Tondo*, Michelangelo's painting of the Holy Family.

"Because we'll never have another chance to see it again so clearly, so unimpeded."

She's been to see it a few times already, because she *adores* Florence and can't seem to stay away from the place, but I hadn't been back in months and months, since even before the quarantine began.

We park on the Arno riverfront, next to the American consulate, and we start walking along the route we always take, with the Ponte Vecchio before us. The city seems to unfold as we walk, revealing glimpses of its noble, distant, exceedingly refined beauty with every step that we take, because there is no city on earth more refined than Florence.

We make an effort not to say, she and I, that there's practically no one walking beside us or around us, but the truth is that there's not a single living soul on Piazza d'Ognissanti, where the Hotel

Excelsior boasts silent pride of place. It was at that extremely de luxe hotel where both our sets of parents bled themselves white to be able to afford to hold their wedding receptions in the midsixties. Next to it is the church of Ognissanti, which nonchalantly houses works by Botticelli and Ghirlandaio, and even Giotto's Ognissanti *Crucifix*.

There's no one at all on the Via della Vigna Nuova and practically nobody, only a very few people indeed, on the Via Tornabuoni, either. They can't be tourists, because the borders are closed, and tourists aren't allowed to enter Italy. They're all Florentines in a hurry, all of them men, and they seem to just be passing through on Via Tornabuoni, as if it might be nothing more than one leg of a route they're following for other reasons, or maybe even a shortcut. They move rapidly along the street, almost furtively, their eyes glued to the pavement ahead of them, without conceding so much as a glance at the buildings, the palazzi, or the boutiques, and in a flash they've scurried away as if they couldn't wait to leave that street behind them, that wonderful street that has always struck me, ever since I was a boy, as the finest thing there is in the world. It is the holy place that marked the culmination of the one and only time I skipped school, at age fourteen, when—with my back to the church of Santi Michele e Gaetano on the Piazzetta degli Antinori, my eyes brimming over with beauty and my heart with enthusiasm for the freedom intrinsic to the act of mischief I was indulging in—I decided that this was the exact proscenium stage upon which a young man of Prato like myself should be able to make himself known to the world. At that point I ducked immediately into the Procacci café to enjoy my very first of those world-famous, extremely expensive, and fantastically delicious truffle paninis that my father had identified to me as the very symbol of the outstanding excellence of that street, and what made it distinct from any other street on earth.

Back then, there was the Bar Giacosa, on Via Tornabuoni, and you could go there to admire gorgeous girls from every corner of the earth—they'd make arrangements to meet each other there toward evening, so they could be courted and wooed by the gangs of neorealistic young men and enjoy an aperitif, when an aperitif was nothing but the start to an evening and not—as it is today—an evening's culminating moment. This was the exceedingly tolerant and gloriously loose and rude Florence of the eighties, when everything seemed possible and entirely permissible, and so everyone did everything. We'd drink and dance and get into fights and sex was everywhere, just ready for you to reach out and grab it, all kinds of sex, and no one was amazed and no one busted your chops about it and no one set themselves up as a judge to visit criticisms upon others.

Also on Via Tornabuoni there was Seeber, the fantastic bookshop with elaborately carved wooden shelves and frescoed vaulted ceilings that both impressed and intimidated me, but at the time I simply told myself that all this beauty and luxury in a bookshop must be there for me, the reader, to remind me just how important I was and how fundamental books themselves were, and how much respect was due them. Because books are for sale, sure, that's true, but they're not *products*, they're not sweaters or ice-cream cones, and so I felt honored to be able to enter that shop, Seeber, as if walking through the front door wasn't an unfettered act that anyone was free to perform (though of course it was), but rather a tacit sign of admission to a club whose one prerequisite for membership was a full understanding of the excellence of literature and art and their basic necessity to life. I never once managed to leave the place without having bought bagsful of books, giving in to the impulse that leads you to poke curiously around, exploring the bookshelves, and persuades you to choose books by authors you've never read before, just because you open a book at random and a formidable line of writing leaps out at you, and there you are, you've been pollinated, and so you grow.

Seeber is gone now, swept aside by Max Mara in the early years of the millennium, when we were still foisting off on an unsuspecting public the comically naïve persuasion that Italian fashion could push the entire country into the future, serving as its symbol and its protective hauberk. Seeber, a shop I still can't quite believe no longer exists. Every time I pass—I don't know what kind of a fool I must be—I just can't seem to keep from peering to see if it might happen to be miraculously open for business once again. Seeber bookshop, which displayed my first novel, *Fughe da fermo* (Standing starts), in the front window in 1995. When I saw it there, with that chilly black-and-white cover with the heart traced on the asphalt that my friend and agent, Sergio Perroni, had come up with, and with that title, also Perroni's creation, the thrill and the excitement was so dizzying that we had to take refuge at Caffè Giacosa, Carlotta and I. I made both her and the bartender laugh when I ordered a glass of cordial.

But today we can stop in the middle of the street to watch Via Tornabuoni flow slowly and then spread wide to become the Piazza Santa Trìnita, hemmed in by sixteenth-century palazzi that in the days of the Medici sometimes served as a handball court, and then it turns gently and terminates in the sublime Santa Trìnita bridge, built by Ammannati to a design by Michelangelo.

We continue to avoid acknowledging the fact, Carlotta and I, that we're strolling through a city that has emptied out, because if we acknowledge it then we're going to have to talk about it, and remember the virus that the Florentines evidently fear, even though that virus has been relatively mild in its effects in Florence, and in Prato, and throughout Tuscany, and on down to the southern end of the Italian boot, certainly much milder than in the gasping North, flat on its collective deathbed, and there's no one who can tell us why.

We try to change the subject—the sweet tantrums and whims of our children, the fate of my mamma, always wide-eyed and dressed in linen, the magnificent accent of the Georgian woman who cares for her, Marina, who also happens to be a music teacher, married to another music teacher, and their children are musicians too, and it must have been the Good Lord Almighty himself who sent her to us. And in the meantime I wonder what could ever happen to fill these streets with crowds again, bring them back to life, and I'm not saying just tourists, but filled with actual Florentines, and I can't help but say and think that it might just be better if Florence remained the way we're seeing it now, beautiful and deserted, a temple, an open-air museum. But if there's a wrong-headed, unsuccessful thought in my head, why it's certainly this one, and if there's an idea that I don't want and I can't embrace, it would be the thought that my future consists of stroll after stroll through a world emptied of people and filled with deserted buildings that, even as they rot and deteriorate, continue telling me the story of their former glories, as if a neutron bomb—that weapon people fantasized about during the Cold War—had gone off, killing all the people while leaving all the buildings intact.

Still, I can't help but wonder whether we might not be facing another of those epochal changes that we must all adjust to, like it or not, however much we may hate it, and we must make our peace with the thought that the hordes of tourists who used to run roughshod over Florence have now become a thing of the past, along with the horse-drawn carriages and the hats and the Walkmans.

In fact, it's possible that tourism itself—at every level, to every destination—is destined to dwindle until it flickers out entirely, because travel is something that can only happen if there's a minimum of faith in the idea that the world is a hospitable place, free of danger, and it's hard to think such a thought after they've locked you up in your own house for months on end and told you that you have to fear other people's respiration and even your own breath. That you could die from a cough and kill with a sneeze and be sick as a dog even if you felt as fit as a fiddle. That it was better for you just to live far from your fellow humans and discourage visits, any and all visits, even including—nay *above all*—visits from children, because the virus did children no harm, people were saying, but children could transmit the virus with chilling efficiency. That it was prudent to put on gloves before touching anything, even your own bed, even your own dinner table; that you had to continually disinfect everything around you; that you had to wash your hands ten times a day because the world, the whole world, and not just the world's air, was infected. That if you were of a certain age—let's say, age sixty-five and up, but even from age sixty on, like most of the tourists that visit Florence and Rome and Venice—and if you then caught the virus, it was far more likely that you'd die than survive.

But I don't want to say any of this to Carlotta. She's an optimist. Like the Mage, like Giovannini. Alongside the evil, she always sees the good, and she's not afraid of change. She doesn't fear the subversion of the status quo; if anything she finds it amusing, and she's never nostalgic for the past. In fact, she has to laugh at the obsession with nostalgia that she so often scolds me for.

She remembers the past fondly, of course, but she never longs for it, however lovely it may have been, and her past and my past have been lovely indeed. She works every day for the immediate present, and she never fears that the future may turn out to be worse: she'll do her utmost to make sure it's not. She's always said jokingly, but not entirely, that my books talk too much about misery and tragedy.

But now here we are on the Piazza della Signoria, and we have the whole Loggia dei Lanzi all to ourselves as we walk past it. Then we enter the Uffizi, and we're practically alone in there too. Once I manage to shake off the obscene idea that's come over me for a moment that even art might become one of those things people will stop going to see, the virus's umpteenth and most illustrious victim, it starts to dawn on me what a vast and daunting miracle and privilege it is to be able to walk *freely* (Carlotta had a point) through all this magnificence, down the long corridors with checkered floors that offer a view of all Florence. Now that there's no smog, the air is so crystal clear that when you step out on the terrace you feel as if you can just reach out and touch the Palazzo Vecchio with your hand. Then we go right up and stand in front of the *Doni Tondo* and we stay there just as long as we please, because there's no one to shove us from behind and pant loudly at us over our shoulders, and it's an incalculable gift, truly, because finally we're able to see and admire something that we'd never before been able to see and admire—Carlotta points out the sublime perfection of each and every detail, the blades of grass that caress the Virgin Mary's bare foot, the faint blue silhouette of the Monte della Verna looming in the distance, a shape that seems to match up with Joseph's shoulders, the proud, icy, incredibly elegant hues of the fabric of their clothing—and little by little I feel myself fill up with harmony and peace and I remain silent because there is nothing that can be said.

After a while, we exchange a glance and decide it's time to leave the museum, and when we walk out onto the deserted Piazza della Signoria, patrolled in vain by lackadaisical, mask-wearing constables, and we head off down a similarly almost-empty Via dei Calzaiuoli, even though the shops are all open for business, I realize that I'm happy for the first time in a long while, and I turn to embrace my wife in the middle of the street.

Billions Coming In

In mid-June, the economy is still frozen in place, like the lives of all the people and the world as a whole, like those bicycle racers I remember seeing on television as a child but haven't seen since, who would remain for long, drawn-out minutes absolutely immobile, locked into an unimaginable equilibrium on the shiny, steep hardwood floors of the velodrome, before bursting into a furious sprint.

Even the companies that have remained open during the quarantine are starting to have to reckon with a new and harsh reality, and many of the businessmen who were pushing so hard to open back up have come to realize that, unbelievably, *it wasn't all that fundamental after all*: their windows open out on a silent, deserted battlefield that seems to stretch out ad infinitum, because while it's true that Italy was one of the first countries to emerge from the lockdown, much of the world is still in its grip, and though very few orders came in during the lockdown, now the orders have dwindled to next to nothing.

Because they're not allowed to travel, they're all there in the company offices, sitting at their desks as if ready to ward off the specter of another lockdown, unable to do much of anything except worry, incredulous that they've reopened into nothingness, incapable of answering the questions about the future that they're being asked by families and workers, disconcerted and discouraged by the news of titanic bankruptcies of global groups that once seemed more durable than bronze itself, terrified by that immense, inconceivable 50 percent drop in annually reckoned revenue that continues to hover over the projections of so many companies, forcing them to lay off workers, firing them when possible, because there's no company on earth that can see its turnover cut in half and continue to employ the same number of staff.

They continuously wonder whether, in the unknowable universe we've just wandered into, their companies—besides becoming unnecessary and noncrucial and non-indispensable, and therefore subject to being shut down from one day to the next, as we've seen—aren't also becoming marginal and obsolete, indeed, pointless. And while some of them are racking their brains to modify their structure in an attempt to slim down, becoming even meaner and leaner but also *greener and more digital*, there are just as many others who are, instead, starting to wonder whether the time hasn't come to just shut down, perhaps using the money that's just arrived in government financing to pay off employees and suppliers and make sure that not a penny goes to those assholes the bankers, now that it's still possible to shut down operations without getting too badly hurt, before slipping away into a long and agonizing decline that will still force them to go out of business later on, on even worse terms, after performing the last, ultimate sacrifice, the noblest and most stupid one—that of sinking your own personal money into your bonfire of a company.

Shops and cafés and restaurants and hotels are open, that's true, but they have no customers. Like the streets of Florence, those of Milan and Rome and Venice and Turin are empty save for the occasional infrequent masked pedestrian, because the truth is that everyone prefers to stay home at this point, where they at least feel safe, and no one has to bear the burden of trying to continue to live a pale imitation of the life we'd been accustomed to, and by now we watch the evening news without the spasmodic focus we used to devote to it—because now that the peak of the pandemic seems to have passed, it's hard to get very excited about the few meaningless scraps of news that filter in.

Even the billions on their way from the European Union manage to excite only the politicians on TV. Even before receiving the money, they are already starting to quarrel about how to spend it, like those shepherds in the children's tale who quarrel bitterly about which cloud they'd send their sheep to graze on, if the whole sky were one giant pasture that belonged to them and them alone.

So few seem willing to remember how, during the lockdown, the government had already handed out a literal mountain of cash to support the economy and the nation's families. All of this created a brand-new deficit, of course, new debt that one day our children will be obliged to repay, and this is cash that doesn't flow into the consumer markets, because Italians, women and men alike, are mistrustful and frightened. So this money, obtained after a thousand difficulties and delays, is deposited in bank accounts and immediately set aside against darker days. As if instead of an emergency subsidy doled out in the expectation that the economy will soon start up again, a crutch for a convalescent, this massive donation to the public was nothing more than a monstrous version of the universal basic income, or citizen's basic income, or whatever you want to call it, decreeing a definitive acceptance of the quintessence of the idea that lies behind any and every act of public largesse, which is to say the rotten illusion that it's possible for everyone to live without working, because after all, the government can just hand out money.

The Mage calls to tell me that the financing he'd applied for had finally arrived, and his Spanish friends have even started giving him a few orders.

"It's not much, Edo, but it all helps. But now we're going to need to see what'll happen come September..."

It's hard, terribly hard, for freelancers too, those millions of people who no longer have formal jobs, or who never had the ability or the desire to join the ranks of the employed and so decided to set up in business for themselves. Many of them are young men and women who graduated from universities after years of study and hard work. People that I've always admired for the way they've bet it all—intrepidly, I have to say, is how I've always characterized them in my mind—on their own abilities and know-how and on the confidence that they were playing a necessary role, indeed a fundamental role, in an economic system undergoing continual change, discovering new needs with every passing day, a system that must regenerate itself on an ongoing basis and that can no longer afford to hire all the staff that it needs.

I've always rooted for the courage with which they face up to the world of work as free and independent individuals, without guarantees but also without bosses above them; the idea of going out into the world (figuratively and otherwise), fostering deep down inside a personal body of knowledge and lore that is so valuable that it can demand and must receive adequate retribution; their ability to organize their work as they please—work all night, if necessary, because they can always sleep the following morning—independently managing every phrase of that labor, including the decision about when to suspend work and for how long, going on vacation whenever they can, of course, but most important of all, *whenever they please.*

As a shocked and retired businessman who came into the plant every morning and gazed at the nineteenth-century line of employees who punched their time cards to start their day, only to scatter to the various departments, and who couldn't help but wonder whether that was really the best way to organize work in a company that produced textiles, I've always viewed with admiration the fervor, and at the same time the lightheartedness, with which freelancers look out at the world, glimpsing an immense place of great potential, filled with opportunities for gainful employment just a click away, seeing them as the protagonists of a future filled with fervid and courageous but reasonable hopes, thousands of miles away from the Italy I knew, which held tight and frantically to the full-time, long-term job.

The pandemic hit them hard too, considering that during the lockdown they can't have invoiced more than pennies. That lightheartedness instantly turned into vulnerability. Many, many loose collaborations were broken off, and no one can say how many of them will come back to life. In order to survive, freelancers did their best to build some bulwark of self-defense. They accepted the 600-euro subsidy the government was offering, and they suspended payment on whatever mortgages they may have taken out. Now they, too, are waiting to see what September will bring.

"I've never felt so useless in my life, or maybe I should say so nonessential," says Elisa Martelli, a young wine-industry consultant. "It's like living in a vacuum."

"So what's happening in the wine business?"

"The same thing that's happening throughout the economy. What's more, keep in mind that in the world of wine, the added problem is that the vintners have wine cellars full to bursting, and not just figuratively. Their barrels and tanks are literally overflowing with unsold wine, and the harvest is drawing nearer every day. What will they do with this fresh vintage of grapes? Where will they put it?"

"Can't they bottle it?"

"Sure, and that's what they'll do. They'll have to. But it's a mess, because there aren't many vineyards that can stock more than their basic productive capacity, and the factories that produce bottles and labels and corks and crates and the metal cages to hold the bottles have been closed during the lock-down, and it hasn't been possible to order any of those items. Plus, labeling a bottle is always a risk, because every country, every importer, requires different kinds of labels, and last of all, or really, most important of all, as of today there are no orders, nor is there any way to deliver wine outside of the country. Finally, just to put the cherry on top, wine in a bottle takes up much more room than wine in a tank or a vat. Where are they supposed to store them, all those bottles?"

My friend Luciano Cimmino, the great Neapoli-tan industrialist whom I met during my time in the Italian parliament, who told me, in a series of texts over quarantine, about certain spectacular com-mercial adventures during the boom years, when he was going to Libya to sell *intimate knitwear, athletic shoes, and panettone*, and to Brazil to buy T-shirts *in Blumenau, a city founded by twenty or so German farmers who arrived there by boat, and where they still celebrate Oktoberfest*, is also living through the limbo of this waiting period.

"With the reopening process, there's been a little bit of a revival, but it mostly involves living, not buy-ing. People have started leaving the house, taking walks, maybe going and getting a drink out before dinner, but they're not really buying…"

He pauses, heaves a sigh, then goes on: "Or maybe I should say that right now they're only buying the bare necessities. But we don't sell necessities, Edoardo, and you know it. What we sell is always something extra. I don't mean it's something superfluous, because that's a word I dislike, but it's certainly something extra. Because you can do without things that aren't strictly necessary, and we've seen that during this quarantine, when we were all shut in at home eating frozen foods…Is that anything like life for an Italian?"

No, I'd like to tell him, *it certainly isn't*. I ask him how the online sector is doing. Did that help him out at all?

"The online sector had a little jolt, sure, but it's not going to be enough. Hybrid work, or working from home, is emptying out the cities. When people are working from home, they stop going to cafés to get an espresso, they stop buying lunch out, they stop window-shopping…And why would they bother to go buy new clothing if they're not going to work? We're all going to be wearing overalls, that's what awaits us…"

"What about the funding, did that come in?"

"Yes," he says after a pause, "yes, it did."

I say nothing, and he goes on: "The world has changed. There's not much we can do about it. We're at the dawn of a new chapter in history, and it's not going to be a pretty one. I think that if things go on like this, eventually we are also going to have to shut down some of our retail outlets and fire some of our workers...But I want to stay optimistic, you know? Over the long term, I'm pretty sure that this will also prove to be a problem that goes away eventually. Did you see that in the month of March alone, Italian citizens deposited sixteen billion euros in their checking accounts? There's money to be spent, and the European Union is going to have to budget something...In any case, wait and see, September is going to be really tough..."

Every time I hear this refrain of "wait until September," more than worrying, I feel a surge of tenderness, it practically brings me to tears, this recurring motif of waiting to see what September brings.

It seems providential, and quintessentially Italian, the idea of putting off the appointment with bad luck until after the holidays and all that fine weather. As if summer might have some sort of magical soothing effect on our traumatized souls. As if the sun and sea and mountains—which during the darkest moments of the pandemic, we've all assumed at least once would be denied us this year— could successfully rid our minds for at least a few weeks of the specter of an evil future that lurks in ambush, ready to tear us limb from limb, sure, but at least until the first of September it's powerless to touch us. Because it's summer, and when it's summer, Italy is bright with sunshine and truly becomes a priceless sparkling jewel. In summer it's the country where the living is better than any place else on earth, a place where there is no way and no desire to really dwell on our coming misfortunes.

Work? I don't have the time.

Money and Perroni

Then summer arrives, the real, hot summer, and in Prato the heat grows ferocious. After noon I can't even think to write, and I don't do much besides read and listen to music and watch movies and lie on my back in bed and stare at the ceiling.

Only about seven in the evening do I start to recover and I go out to water the scorched plants. Direct summer sunshine is good for the agave plants and certain palm trees, but it's bad for almost all the others, and it's always a big surprise to see how quick they are to recover, especially the weeds, if watered at considerable length.

I don't really know why I want to stay at home while Carlotta and the kids are at the beach, and when she calls to ask me about it, I reassure her that everything's fine, and I'll join them in a few days. *Sure, of course, I know it's the end of July.*

In the incessant rough seas of useless thoughts that surge and ebb in my mind, the only clear thought is the way that in the many past days of suspended animation, the economy increasingly appears to me as a living, all-too-human science, certainly the best-suited of all the disciplines to narrate the substance of our lives and the fervor of our dreams and the misery of our fears: a stupefying generator of stories and hopes, light-years away from the razor-sharp, icy chill of numbers that are usually the medium used to tell that tale.

Because the numbers on inflation, unemployment, the growth or decline of GDP, and tax evasion aren't just numbers, empty percentages. They're photographs, or perhaps paintings that depict both the country and us, the people who live in it.

The account statements from our bank accounts and our credit cards and our debit cards, the positive or negative balance sheets of our checking accounts, the certifications of our mortgages and loans, even our tax returns, strike me as so many chapters of a book or scenes from a film, given the way they manage to recount with a precision worthy of Raymond Carver our economic and financial situations, that is to say our lives.

They're stories, if you know how to read them, and they explain who we are. They testify to where we come from, and they can even predict where we're likely to wind up, because it's easy to say that money doesn't count, and there are plenty of other things that count in life, if you read the biographies and the correspondence of the great poets and novelists—Dylan Thomas and F. Scott Fitzgerald among those closest to us in time, but also that supreme squanderer of money, Baudelaire; and Balzac and Foscolo and Joyce; and William Blake and Daniel Defoe, who are buried side by side in London, in the cemetery of Bunhill Fields, "the Campo Santo of the Dissenters": practically all the classics we venerate—you'll notice that they almost never talk about winged sentiments and great passions, and almost always carp on and on about their lack of money, the expenses that can't be put off any longer but that are also unaffordable, extravagances they bitterly regret, ailing wives and mothers, mouths to feed, children to dress and send to school, miserable hovels they're about to be evicted from. You read them as they beg and plead, the great writers, asking their mothers and fathers and friends and family and guardians and agents and publishers to send them a little something, even a bare pittance, just to help them make it to the end of the coming month, or the next book.

Because when the end of the month does finally roll around, it's a great comfort for each and every one of us to receive a paycheck, and a great and disconcerting ordeal not to, and there's not one among us whose heart doesn't leap up at the news that an invoice issued some time before has now been paid. There's no one who doesn't kick themselves for having contracted this or that debt or, plural, debts, that month by month gnaw away at what little—because it always seems agonizingly little—we've worked so excruciatingly hard to earn.

But even more important than people's jobs is the quantity of money that we have in our wallet or checking account, and the more or less legitimate expectation of more money to come in the future, and the nagging fear that we might not be able to keep up with the mortgage payments on the house we live in, or the lease on the car that we're driving, or the business loans that we took because we needed money, for fuck's sake, that determines the way we live our lives, what we feel we can or cannot do.

It is also money that determines our state of mind and our thoughts, that allows us to love life instead of hating it, that allows a young couple to decide to have children or else forgo them, and it is the lack of money that wickedly suggests to a bankrupt entrepreneur that it's better to commit suicide than live on in shame.

I'd deeply enjoy being able to reason about this with my friend Sergio Perroni, who a little over a year ago decided to leave this world by shooting himself in the head in the presence of the sublime spectacle of the sea and the sky in his beloved town of Taormina. There were few people in this world whom I respected and admired as much as I respected and admired him.

We argued frequently, because it was even kind of cool to argue with Perroni, and there was no reason to take offense for his inevitable instances of insolence, like the time that, in 1996, after the publication of my second, overhasty novel, *Ride con gli angeli* (He laughs with the angels), he sent me a fax stating that he no longer wished to represent me as my literary agent because, *as we've seen, you're strictly a one-book writer*, and he'd concluded that letter with a horrible *Over and out*, which had deeply struck my father, who had read the whole fax—since Perroni had sent the fax to the woolen mill, and not to the house—and had then brought the sheet of paper to me without uttering a word, seeing in it a blazing confirmation of his worst fears about the writing career—let's call it that—that I was undertaking and that, to hear him tell it, was threatening to steal time and energy from the other career, as a businessman, that my father had chosen for me.

They met once, my babbo and Perroni, the only time he came to visit me in Prato, when *Fughe da fermo* came out, the only book that he said I had in me and the only one I had ever written at that point. He only stayed for a few hours, because he had to hurry back to Taormina to finish translating Houellebecq, but I recall clearly how much he liked Babbo.

They spoke at length, but I never did find out about what, and when I took him to the station, Sergio told me that Babbo resembled Lee Marvin, the great American actor who made so many Westerns. When I told him that, Babbo sat rapt in thought for a few seconds, and then replied that no one had ever said such a thing to him before—because when he was young Babbo resembled Clark Kent, and in fact all his friends called him NemboKid—Italian for Superman—but then added *actually, that might work. Lee Marvin might work.*

Perroni wrote divinely, and he translated, if anything, even better. No one—*no one*—translated like he did, and he often amused himself by signing his work with a pen name—Vincenzo Vega.

The times that we argued hardest were the ones when he said things like this: "When all is said and done, all you ever wrote about was money." One day I retorted that he didn't understand a fucking thing, because—and this is what I said—*it's always the deterioration of the economic welfare of the middle class that points to the changes of society and perhaps of History itself,* and he told me to go fuck myself and snickered when he heard me mention History, and I hung up on him in a rage. But those were and remain the lessons that I need, the ones that wind up in swordplay, and now that I'm here on the terrace of my own home feeling the first cool breeze of this torrid day on my flesh and reading the texts that Perroni and I exchanged over the years, I find one that I'd sent him from a bookstore asking him for advice about what book to read. He'd immediately replied, "Xenophon's *Anabasis* and Victor Hugo's *The Man Who Laughs*, but only in Luigi Tenconi's translation."

A few seconds later he added, *Saber strokes of beauty every three lines or so.*

Rise and Fall

And then August arrives, and I, too, go to the beach, and incredibly, *there it is, the summer,* and it's the Italian summer, the same as it's always been. In fact, if possible, in a certain sense it's even more Italian than ever, because most of the people who would usually have gone on vacation in some other country stayed home this year. And now they're packing the beaches. Sardinia, the Aeolian Islands, Sicily, Ponza—all the islands, whether big or little, are packed to bursting.

I never know what to do when I'm on the beach, but I try to stay there as long as I possibly can. I get there around 9:30 in the morning, when you can read in peace and quiet, and then, after having a meal at home that's anything but frugal, I come back around three in the afternoon and stay until the sun goes down, when girls and boys go running down to the water's edge to take pictures of the setting sun and post them on Instagram.

And then, one morning when I've woken up early and arrived on the beach while the lifeguards are still busy raking and grooming the sand, I lazily start poking through the archives of the *New York Times* on my cell phone. I stumble across a magnificent review that Paul Krugman chose to write in 2016 of *The Rise and Fall of American Growth*, a book about economic development that the op-ed columnist— and 2008 Nobel laureate in economics—called "a magisterial combination of deep technological history, vivid portraits of daily life over the past six generations and careful economic analysis."

I immediately buy the book, convinced not so much by the lavish praise but rather by the faint hesitation I detect toward the end of the review: the few lines in which Krugman seems genuinely stirred by the arguments of the learned scholar, but uncertain whether to refute them or embrace them in full, perhaps because the author, Robert J. Gordon, renowned and respected macroeconomist and professor of Social, Political, and Economic Sciences at Northwestern University, outside of Chicago, has impressive things to say, starting from the introduction to his own book:

Economic growth is not a steady process that creates economic advance at a regular pace, century after century. Instead, progress occurs much more rapidly in some times than in others. There was virtually no economic growth for millennia until 1770, only slow growth in the transition century before 1870, remarkably rapid growth in the century ending in 1970, and slower growth since then. Our central thesis is that *some inventions are more important than others*, and that the revolutionary century after the Civil War was made possible by a unique clustering, in the late nineteenth century, of what we will call the "Great Inventions."

The Great Inventions—under that umbrella term, Gordon groups electricity, running water, the construction of sewer systems in major cities, chemistry and its applications to pharmacology, the internal combustion engine, and such modern systems of communications as the telegraph and the telephone and the radio. They are the extraordinary technological achievements that arrive more or less all at once about three-quarters of the way through the nineteenth century and find immediate practical application and widespread popular adoption, triggering a technological revolution that successfully "improved the standard of living of the vast majority of Americans in ways previously unimaginable"—only to be followed a few decades later by other inventions and the formidable leaps forward that sprang out of them: among them automobiles, television, electric appliances, air travel, and air-conditioning, whose further, incredibly powerful, decades-long thrust created what Gordon calls "the Special Century," which he places between 1870 and 1970.

I put down the massive, 762-page hardcover that had been delivered to me in what seemed like a blink of the eye, a book that I can't guess how many readers ever bothered to bring to the beach, and I smile.

I've always been deeply pleased by the idea that a breakthrough does not necessarily have to be followed by a miserable, flagging decline and a return to its preexisting state of calm and quiet, but rather by another breakthrough of equal or greater power and duration that completely transforms the nature of the effort, making it different and better. It's a bit like the way that when I was a young man I could make love twice in a row, or with boxing's one-two punch, a rapid combination of two blows; the most illustrious and formidable one-two punch having been unleashed by Muhammad Ali—my absolute idol in my youth and for the rest of my life, and for all time, whose biography I read over and over when I was a boy because I wanted to imitate him and become the world heavyweight champion. The recipient of that one-two punch was George Foreman in Kinshasa, Zaire: a huge wide left hook that could safely be described as a wild swing and that laid back on the ropes that Texan Hercules, tired by now after all the punches that he landed against Ali in the previous rounds without obtaining any detectable effect, and the most precise and devastating hard right ever seen in the history of boxing!

I'm immediately remained of another one-two punch, the one delivered by the system of propulsion employed by the Apollo space program. In fact, if you stop to think about it, that one resulted in not a double but a *triple* ignition of the Saturn V, the three-stage rocket of unrivaled power that upon liftoff from the launch platform consumed fifteen tons of fuel per second. Just five years before Muhammad Ali's sublime KO, and therefore at the absolute zenith of the Special Century, the rocket carried the Apollo 11 capsule with its first stage to an altitude of thirty-eight miles and then detached to fall back to earth's surface. At that same point, however, the second stage ignited, blasting the capsule straight up to an altitude of 110 miles, at a velocity of 15,000 miles per hour, whereupon it too ran out of fuel and fell back to earth in its turn, allowing for the ignition of the third stage, the stage that decreed ultimate victory in that proud challenge to the cruel enemy, gravity, and its wicked sister, entropy, a duel that the Americans won on behalf of all mankind, but especially for me, because I not only wanted to become a boxer but also an astronaut, and that booster proceeded to launch into orbit a manned capsule that weighed more than fifty tons. From its perch in orbit it then proceeded to sail effortlessly to the moon with three astronauts crammed inside and then returned to earth, by God, equipped with a computer far less powerful than a present-day cell phone.

And then it dawns on me how these two so exceedingly American moments happened more or less at the turn of the seventies, as if they were the swan song of that Special Century that, according to Gordon, was just then beginning to lose its impetus and fade.

That's right, because now we're coming to the most interesting and horrifying part of *The Rise and Fall of American Growth*.

Basing his work on the statistical evidence of industrial production, Gordon states that the development of society and the economy that springs out of the arrival of the Great Inventions was sudden and dizzying and so durable that it seemed interminable, but above all it was incomparably greater than anything that would come in the following decades— the years of the computer age and the digital revolution, the era of Bill Gates and Steve Jobs and the workshops in Silicon Valley garages where their companies first saw the light, and then the years of the internet and unbroken global communication: the years we lived online, the years of smartphones, apps, and social networks.

Gordon writes that what we witnessed from 1970 on was a much less powerful and far more selective arc of development:

> Advances since 1970 have tended to be channeled into a narrow sphere of human activity having to do with entertainment, communications, and the collection and processing of information. For the rest of what humans care about—food, clothing, shelter, transportation, health, and working conditions both inside and outside the home—progress slowed down after 1970, both qualitatively and quantitatively.

The professor concludes that the Special Century is therefore a singular event, with a beginning and an end—a never-to-be-seen-again occurrence in human history, because so many of its conquests could only happen once—while everything else that's happened since is nothing more than the refinement of well-known technologies, even though at times those refinements may have in some cases been quite extreme, and the impact of those refinements on the world is nothing more than a distant echo—the residual background radiation, we might say, if we're willing to persist in using astronomical metaphors—of that epochal economic boom of which we'll never have a chance to witness the second coming, because it's impossible to invent electricity again, any more than it is the telephone and penicillin and the internal combustion engine.

The advent of, first, computers and then the internet has certainly changed the world and created new and unimaginable opportunities for development and growth, Gordon concedes. But with data in hand he claims that development has not brought humanity anything remotely comparable to the progress and prosperity and high employment of the Special Century, which means that our author foresees for the middle class and for the American economy as a whole a perpetuation of the substantial stagnation that is currently gripping them already. The reason is that the slowing of technological progress in such vast areas of the experience of human life coincides with an uptick in the growth of inequality, a decline in levels of education, and the aging of the American population.

Now, I do understand—Enrico Giovannini has just patiently explained it to me in the umpteenth phone call that I made to him, treacherously, from the shade of my beach umbrella—that what Gordon has to say is based on GDP statistics, which means that it inevitably leaves out everything that the GDP fails to measure: the pollution of the planet, global warming, an entire continent abandoned to its own devices, the marginalization of significant portions of the world's population, the quality and quantity of the world's welfare and prosperity, the immense body of work done by volunteers and nonprofits, and then civil rights crushed underfoot and endless expanses of poverty and famines and migrations and diseases and dictatorships and, above all, unhappiness.

I know that, and for what my opinion is worth, I too believe that we ought to start measuring the economy with a different, better system. One that takes into account more than just the numbers that make up a nation's GDP—that is to say, the consumption of individuals, the investments of companies and those same individuals, public spending, and net exports. No, we should measure the impact on the world that these numbers and business decisions ultimately will have.

I know, it get it all, but can you really say that Gordon is wrong?

It's true that our cell phones are devices of wonder, and that all it takes nowadays is a couple of clicks to buy a house, but automobiles continue to be nothing more than the latest and ultimate reworking of the horse-drawn carriage: we've eliminated the team of six horses and replaced it with an internal combustion engine that in the overwhelming majority of motorized vehicles on the planet burns gasoline or diesel fuel, according to mechanical operating principles that were patented around the end of the nineteenth century, while the gases and dusts that are spewed out are carcinogenic, working their way into our lungs and slowly killing us. Trains are still the same old iron or steel conveyances they always have been, contraptions that were invented around the middle of that same nineteenth century, and they still run at greater or lesser speeds on steel rails laid out across the countryside. Airplanes, moreover, are by far the most disappointing of all means of transport: since they retired the Concorde, which at least went fast and spanned the world in a truly impressive manner, we've had to settle for these oversized long-distance buses with wings and jet engines fastened onto their sides, which still take nine hours to get from Rome to New York—even the latest generation of airliners, where we're crammed in like sardines—nine hours, exactly the same amount of time as the Boeing 707 or the propeller-driven DC-7s of the sixties.

To heat our homes, we still set something flammable on fire, just like primitive humans did when they lived in caves, and our furnaces and boilers are even more retrograde than our car engines—they are infinite numbers of times worse when it comes to the way they pollute the atmosphere.

Every day we eat and drink chemical garbage, and at this point it's a losing battle to try to avoid that junk in mass-market foodstuffs, to say nothing of GMOs.

In the sixties, we already lived in houses illuminated by electric light, with central heating, natural gas, running water, sewer hookups, radios, and a television set; today, sixty years later, we've only added the products of the development that arrived after the Special Century, namely, computers and internet.

What's more, and most importantly of all, in the world today there are more than two billion people who work all day for a crust of bread, basically, in Dickensian conditions, in comical but ultimately tragic contempt of any and all notion of workers' rights, battles that were fought in the evil and capitalist West.

Many of these underpaid workers are being despicably exploited so that you and I can save a few dollars on the price of a dress or a cotton shirt that our sons and daughters can afford to buy, brand-new, every Saturday afternoon because they cost so little, only to throw them out after wearing them once or at the very most twice, in obedience to the dictates of that obscene philosophy of fast fashion—a ridiculous, fucked-up concept that I distinctly recall being hailed with jubilation by the advocates of free markets when it first appeared, with that incredible watchword, "Never twice on Instagram," a slogan designed to make anyone who continues to wear an item after posting a picture of them wearing it feel like a complete loser. And who even cares what becomes of that shirt or dress once it's been discarded? I can tell you where it winds up, it winds up in Kenya, in a street market—and clothing that no one even bothers to try selling winds up in immense and brightly colored dumps. Every so often someone comes through and sets fire to all that clothing, those gigantic heaps of rags that plenty of imbeciles stubbornly insist on calling "fashion."

A Personal Matter

There's another reason why Gordon's words ring profoundly true to me, and as if they were my own words. As Sergio Vari said, these are personal matters.

It was around the middle of the nineties, when everything miraculously still seemed to be holding together, that I first heard someone say that this period we were living in was a time of enormous decline.

The person who told me so was my father-in-law, Sergio Carpini, a volcano of a man who amassed a considerable fortune by inventing and selling fabrics to designers and who made a point of always saying immediately exactly what he thought about things. Like that time in the late sixties that he asked the artist Lucio Fontana during a very fancy Milan dinner party why he kept making all those slashes in his canvases, after the initial inspiration that drove him to do the first one and present it to the world. What was he planning to do, anyway, set up a production line and become an industrial manufacturer himself?

The progress of humanity, Carpini maintained, had ground to a definitive halt the day that a world-renowned fashion designer asked him how much his fabrics cost—and not the discount, let's be very clear on this point, he'd asked the actual price—because if world-famous fashion designers, who had more millions than they knew what to do with and who transformed his fabrics into articles of clothing that they then proceeded to sell for their weight in gold all around the world started thinking about skimping on the costs of their raw materials, then it really did mean that it was all over.

If human ingenuity wasn't being rewarded as it deserved and was forced to kneel to the stingy and peevish recommendations of accountants and bean counters, Carpini opined, then not only did this spell the death of Italian fashion, but also the very spirit of artisanal creativity, with its accompanying retinue of machinery and the sweat of worker's brows, and the full occupation and universal prosperity that it tended to spread. It meant undermining the very foundations of the future.

The death of fashion was near, he felt, if a customer started to cut into the fair remuneration that a craftsman—because he liked to refer to himself as a craftsman, even though he'd become a wealthy man, sure, but infinitely less wealthy than the designers he worked for—ought to be paid. Because a craftsman needs that pay to continue to survive and work, experimenting and exploring all the wrong turns and unsuccessful approaches that he could, if he wanted to. Because that's the nature of innovation, you get it wrong and you get it wrong again and you get it wrong again and again, until you finally stumble across the right idea, at which point any and all losses are promptly covered and forgotten about.

In any case, that's right, sooner or later the client was bound to start cutting into that fair remuneration, and eventually the client would completely disregard that understanding about pay because now the client needed to pay off the incredibly costly army of consultants that he'd hired to help him cut costs, and given the fact that *where there's no earning there's bound to be losses*, by the end of a few more years, it would all have gone up in smoke. First the unfettered inventiveness of the craftsman, and then craftsmanship itself, and with the disappearance of craftsmanship, the textiles industry as a whole, and with the textiles industry, Italy itself, and with Italy, the world at large.

This story becomes more significant and less amusing as time goes by. Carpini no longer seems like an object of fun, an overblown catastrophist, and instead becomes a foul-mouthed oracle who glimpsed a future so grim that it scared him, so much so that he sold his company, at the time still prosperous and profitable, and retired to the harsh soil of the Chianti d'Arezzo to make wine.

Back then, I wasn't entirely in agreement with him on his view that, if his customers dared to ask him how much his products cost, instead of just hurrying up to buy them enthusiastically the way they had in the past, then that meant that the world had entered into a phase of irremediable decline. We frequently argued.

I couldn't see it as possible, any more than I could imagine it as a realistic outcome: the end of craftsmanship. The facts on the ground flew in the face of such a concept. We were craftsmen ourselves, and in order to sell our fabrics, which had less inventive flair and were more solidly traditional than Carpini's, we'd always been forced to battle against our competitors—competitors that he practically didn't even have. We certainly didn't expect our customers to ask us for discounts, but we were the ones who *offered* the discounts. That said, though, in those years Lanificio T. O. Nesi & Figli was roaring along like an express train, and thanks in part to the periodic, providential devaluations of the Italian lira, the company was presenting the fattest, rosiest balance sheets in its history.

The respect I felt was due to Carpini kept me from telling him so, but I thought he was just getting old and no longer had the ability—or simply no longer had the desire—to manage to understand the ways in which the world was changing. To keep from getting into an ugly quarrel with my wife's father, I would always make an effort to not say anything when he started spouting about the world having "lost its way home." Aside from any discussions we might have about business and economics, he was a man I truly liked.

The few times I happened to have gotten up on the wrong side of the bed, though, I'd fight back, rising in a mock-heroic pose of comic defense of the traitorous times I'd grown up in, summoning modernism to stand as my shield man and bragging about the achievements of free-market capitalism. It was the same free-market capitalism which in those days I considered myself to be on the very diamond-hard cutting edge of, poor fool that I was. After all, I told myself, we were a small and independent corporation, operating freely and moving with rapidity and agility, proudly exporting Italian products, and sinking our historic roots in the manufacturing tradition of the industrial West while making use of the most advanced techniques of production. We were producing a venerable old material, true, woolen fabrics, but at levels of extremely high quality, and we were selling it to the clothing manufacturers of the richest country on earth, that very same magnificent Germany, where every taxi driver seemed to own a Mercedes, especially and notably in the part of Germany where our clients' factories were located, factories and plants that were never new and gleaming and that had never been graced by the gaze of a starchitect. They were always furnished and decorated poorly at best, and yet they still represented the fulcrum of a little-known textile system, one that was rarely if ever mentioned in the mass media, but that was very powerful indeed. This textile manufacturing sector in Germany had done nothing since postwar reconstruction but grind out profits by selling understated, sobersided woolen overcoats and dress jackets and heavy jackets for those millions of women and men who lived there, in the center of Europe, and who couldn't care less about "fashion."

Then Carpini really lost his temper. He told me I hadn't understood a fucking thing, and insisted on the vast decline that he was seeing everywhere he turned—*How the fuck can you be blind to it, Edoardo*?—and from then on it was one curse word after another. Then, carried away with that emphasis and fury that had always haunted him and driven him to be a success in life, he'd start shaking his head and talking to himself, answering his own question to the tune of, why sure, of course I couldn't see the decadence because *I'd been born within the very bounds of that decadence*, me and all the others of my generation, and in fact in my lifetime I'd never known anything *other* than decadence.

At Their Very Best

All around me, everyone is enjoying that summer as it proceeds, under the beneficent rays of one lovely, unshakable sunny day after another, and to look at it from the beach of Forte dei Marmi, it really does seem as if the virus doesn't exist, and never has.

People are sunbathing, strolling along the water's edge, swimming, hugging each other delightedly, greeting each other like long-lost friends, lobbing balls back and forth with those damned beach rackets. Yet all the same in their eyes and in their gestures, I seem to sense the vibration of a feverish fervor and the anxious and obstinate determination to go on living as if nothing had happened, for as long as they could possibly keep it up, because by now there's no mistaking the fact that the virus is still around, it hasn't dissipated with the warm weather and the summer sun, the way some people said it would, and the infections are still spreading, and I can't wait for it to be time to go and pick up my son Ettore, the young bon vivant who's just decided to get out of Sardinia scant seconds before the vacationers managed to infect him with Covid. Ettore is due to land at Pisa airport around sunset, aboard the last flight, our family's last fleeting hope.

As I wait before setting out, I think about how surprising and comical and in fact truly decadent it is that, in 1996, Carpini and I should have plunged into such overheated arguments about topics that we thought were abstract and to which we were somehow impervious, when all the while the wave was swelling and building, the same wave that just a few years later would sweep away our little companies, and thousands of little sister companies, and only served to pump up—more and more, relentlessly, grotesquely, disproportionately, obscenely— the balance sheets of the fucking fashion designers.

Who knows why I persisted so stubbornly in telling him he was wrong, that formidable father-in-law

I'd lucked into, when actually his words scalded me internally like the sips of that 120-proof whiskey that I once loved to drink by the idiotic glassful, and which dropped hook, line, and sinker down into the dark pool of my most secret turmoil.

That's right, because I began to believe it when I was just a kid, back in the bad old days of Italian austerity, when we were careful to turn off the lights in our houses, and the streetlights were left dark, and no one was allowed to take their cars out of the garage on Sunday. What I believed was that something necessary and fundamental had vanished from the world I knew, and sometimes at night I'd remain awake just thinking about it, until I understood that being young meant finding yourself continuously rocked and shuttled back and forth between horrendous fears and immense delightful euphorias, and the only way to survive was to resign myself to the idea that I was going to have to live every day of my life in the throes of incomprehensible and terrifyingly powerful forces that seemed to find it amusing to toss me roughly from one state of mind to another. When I understood that, I simply stopped worrying, in part because I was growing up in the best Italy ever, and life was sweeter than honey.

That lurking sensation of loss, though, never entirely left me, and no illumination ever arrived to explain it. It struck me that I might have come close now and again in the books I've written, but I've still never managed to clarify it even to myself, because every attempt to analyze it rationally crumbles immediately into the dust of personal experience and memory, whereas if, instead, I try to tell the story through fictional narrative, it only winds up fading and getting tangled up with nostalgia, as Svetlana Boym and the magnificent Zygmunt Bauman have so clearly explained to us—and indeed, once, thanks to the good offices of Elisabetta Sgarbi, I had the immense good fortune of meeting Bauman. I was the opening act of a summer evening's entertainment at the Polytechnic University of Milan, which included his eagerly awaited master class on *Retrotopia*, which had just been published, and while we waited to listen raptly to what indeed proved to be a master class of blinding acuity and clarity, I read to the audience of distracted young students a passage about passion and sex from my book *Infinite Summer*, and I had the impression that the reading revived them at least a little from the grueling heat and, from the way I saw him chat with the translator and nod as I read, it may have even piqued Maestro Bauman's interest—so as I was saying, nostalgia is quite another matter, and if you read their books, you'll understand that immediately.

But actually, as I drive down the half-empty superhighway toward Pisa's Galilei airport, it finally seems to dawn on me what I felt I was missing then and what I feel I'm missing now.

It's not the past.

It's not my own wonderful and joyous childhood, spent reading science fiction until sleep forced my eyes shut. It's not my teenage years, the adolescence that it now seems to me I wasted miserably, suffering like a dog as I yearned for girls who inexplicably failed to reciprocate my desires, and I sought the only consolation I could hope for in Billy Joel and Bruce Springsteen. Not my reckless youth, the years that followed, when as a young man, I stretched and stretched the limits until the rope gave way and finally what saved my life was marrying Carlotta, twenty-seven long years ago, when I finally devoted myself to writing with some minimum level of commitment and concentration, so that my first child and my first novel came into the world more or less at the same time, in May 1995, when, in fact, everything miraculously still seemed to be holding together.

Although I firmly believe—in fact, I find the thought enchanting—that it's possible and indeed common to miss something you've never experienced, it's not even someone else's past that I miss: that earlier era, calmer and more relaxed, less hasty and less cutting, and yet more fruitful, that Babbo always told me about.

What I missed was—and still is—the future that Gordon's Special Century promised us, and which never came true.

The future in which science and technology would never stop and Great Inventions would continue to arrive, new discovery after new discovery, solving people's problems, whether practical or deeply human, freeing them from slavery and humiliation, lifting from the shoulders of men and especially women the weightier burdens of life that they were—and always have been—obliged to accept and carry, setting our sights on eliminating the restrictions we're born with and have coexisted with for millennia, in an attempt to get past them once and for all.

It was nothing but a promise, of course, but its foundations were well established in reality, in the present. And in Italy too.

Because in the fifties, Gordon's Special Century had arrived in Italy too, lifting back up onto its feet a country that had been felled to its knees by Fascism and the war, creating out of nothing a vibrant and even frantic economy, largely made up of tiny artisanal companies that had given jobs to millions of people who had previously been laboring in the fields, beginning to spread a providential rivulet of shared prosperity that had then continued to flow for decades, ultimately making Italy one of the wealthiest and most highly industrialized countries on earth just as I was growing into a boy. I became aware of all this because, living as I did in Prato, I happened to be in one of the key geographic locations for this entire process. To the soundtrack of pounding looms I glimpsed a formidable system for raising people and nations that was based on science and technology and began by introducing innovation to defeat poverty and abolish ancient and brutal, beastly duties, ultimately unleashing the claims and determination of human rights and ensuring their achievement. Because that is what economic growth really is at its finest: a benevolent and blessed mechanism that continuously creates new jobs available to everyone, not just for college graduates or even high school graduates, but *everyone*, and even in the context of the greatest possible imaginable development of innovation and in the maximum reliance on the use of machinery, there was still no shortage of jobs for human beings, in those days, and it became true, in fact spellbindingly true, what is no longer true today, so that anyone who still says it is nothing better than a fool—namely, that innovation creates jobs.

What I missed was a future in which it was possible to dream while fully wide awake, a future devoid of any limits, save the limits of imagination itself, in which we could hope to fight against the evils of this world—yes, yes indeed—beginning with the possibility of doing without petroleum and replacing it with something entirely different, thus making it possible to ensure that cars and trucks and airplanes and ships and any and every other means of motorized transportation and even boilers in apartment buildings would no longer pollute the air that we breathe. There would be an inexhaustible source of energy, at zero cost, available to everyone, and we'd live in a world where it would just be fun never to turn a city's lights off, even in the wee hours of the night, because by keeping them on we wouldn't run up any kind of electric bill—though every once in a while, we'd turn them off, just so we could see the stars.

A future in which we'd found a way to get rid of plastic, to cleanse the sea and the air of all the toxins and poisons we'd dumped into them, a way to conquer all diseases for all time, because that's what science and technology do, at their very best: they help—indeed, they serve—humanity at large.

A contagious future that drove the visionaries who wrote about science fiction and made science fiction movies to date their books and films just a few dozen years in the future, and to imagine a world that would possess spaceships and robots and teletransportation and all the other wonders that we haven't come even close to achieving; a world where, in 2019, replicants would work for us in off-world colonies, where they would see attack ships on fire off the shoulder of Orion.

The future that kept me up at night when I was a kid, the future at whose center—at whose heart, actually—lay progress.

That's what I miss, I think to myself, as Ettore emerges, handsome as the noonday sun, from Pisa airport. I'm waiting outside because a brusque, masked watchman refused to even let me enter the building in compliance with the new, stricter anti-virus regulations, leaving me there to stand in the gathering dusk, surrounded by a few other people waiting with me, and like me, for one of the very few flights scheduled to land that day.

That future, as well as the history of that future.

The World's Fair

We hug and plant kisses on each other's cheeks, me and my young son, because if he's caught the virus, then I want to catch it too. Then we drive away together into a magnificent sunset that silences us both for a while, and then Ettore tells me that he's been wanting to hear The Boss sing "No Surrender."

So I put it on the stereo immediately and we sing it together, "No Surrender," and then we sing other Springsteen songs after that, the songs that he wants, "Spirit in the Night," "Dancing in the Dark," "Bobby Jean," which when all is said and done, like all the Boss's songs, despite the frantic rhythm and pacing, are often basically sad songs that tell the story of a loss. I wonder whether now is the right time to tell Ettore about it, this story of the future that never came about, but which did reach a culminating moment, a point at which it emerged from the ideas and illustrations and books and took on a life of its own, offering itself as our potential reality, set forth to the world in all its pomp and circumstance.

That story, an American story, of course, deeply American, began in New York, with a giant knowing wink to literature, when a hasty and furious reclamation project quickly transformed the thousand-plus acres of the immense Valley of Ashes that the characters of *The Great Gatsby* drive by in their custom convertible automobiles as they head off to drink and dance the night away in Manhattan—because it was on that very site that the World's Fair was going to be inaugurated, on April 30, 1939, just four short months before that dickhead Hitler invaded Poland.

The theme of the World's Fair was "Building the World of Tomorrow," and the fair housed the pavilions of sixty different nations—including Italy, which had one of the most widely admired pavilions, with water running down its facade. It became the ideal stage set for the great American corporations of the time, which as they emerged from the Great Depression, placed all their bets on the industrial design that in those years had just come into being. They laid all their chips on their certainty that only the brand-new canon of beauty contained in the flowing lines and curved surfaces of industrial design could awaken the optimism of consumers, helping to sell their products, whatever those products might be.

And so those corporations took up the concept of streamlining as the symbol of a future in which everything could and would have to be reimagined in both form and substance, with the application of that discipline to dozens of ordinary objects in everyday use: from toothbrushes to portable radios, from cars to vacuum cleaners, from sewing machines to refrigerators, all the way up to locomotives and ocean liners, modifying their appearance so profoundly that they seemed to be gifts from a brave new world, audacious and already here, on our doorstep, redesigning the present and catapulting it toward a road stretching into the future, a road without a visible end, leading toward gleaming, daring years when we'd go from place to place not in earthbound cars, but in flying machines of various description and when the cities would bristle with skyscrapers reaching straight up a mile or more.

At the center of the fair, two great structures arose: the Perisphere, a sphere 180 feet across, and the Trylon, a triangular pylon 610 feet high, both of them gleaming white, and everywhere, as far as the eye could see, were fountains, fluorescent lights, towers and palaces of every inspiration and shape, flanking the immense pavilions of the major corporations, revealing to gasping crowds the *World of Tomorrow.*

General Motors presented Futurama, an attraction outside of which stretched seemingly endless lines of fairgoers eager to board one of the 600 moving theater seats with individual speakers that transported visitors along a route around a large-scale model, covering an expanse of 36,000 square feet and depicting the world of 1960, at the time just twenty years in the future, when the cities would be dazzlingly clean, crisscrossed with broad boulevards down which zoomed cars with daring silhouettes, surrounded by unspoiled parklands, in turn crisscrossed with seven-lane superhighways intersecting across bridges and overpasses that were both graceful and exceedingly ambitious.

The World's Fair was visited by millions and millions of people. It left such a powerful and lasting impression on the hearts and minds of Americans that they really thought that *that* was it, the future that awaited them: an immense future of boundless potential, naïve and even childish in the unattainable perfection that it identified as America's ultimate destination. No run-down slums in Futurama, no poverty—an ideal that was absolutely irresistible to the pride and sky-high morale of the world's greatest superpower, which in just a few short years would emerge triumphant from a war whose devastation was wrought elsewhere, supported by an intact and mighty economy, ready to flood Europe with its products, a Europe whose factories lay in ruins.

The World's Fair resonates and thrums in the thirty or so pages that adorn the finale of *World's Fair*, E. L. Doctorow's prodigious novel of 1985, which recounts the life of a young Jewish boy in the 1930s who lives and grows up with his family in a Bronx that in those years was a quiet and dignified place. It culminates with his visit to the World's Fair—and you really ought to read it, if you still have the desire to thrill to the story of a boy learning about what life is really like as he grows up, if you're still willing and ready to abandon yourself to the slow and ultimately human unfolding of a dazzling story of the minor details of life, lulled by the masterful narrative descriptions of an extraordinary author, by the skilled embrace of a talented storyteller who takes on the vast task of describing through a child's eyes the sheer discovery of life, magically turning us into that child.

It's a magnificent novel, *World's Fair*, the kind you want to read no more than twenty pages a day of, because you can't stand the idea of it ending, so you nibble away at it a little at a time, saving the best hours of the day for reading it. It's a book studded with pearls.

The slow progress of the monumental truck that sprayed the asphalt with clouds of iridescent water at sunset on a summer day! Those few perfect pages dedicated to the rustling flutter of the *Hindenburg* over Edgar's house, as he chases it admiringly all through the Bronx, laughing all the way, a symbol of that very Nazism that promised death to boys like him—although what would die, just a few days later, was none other than the *Hindenburg* itself, its tons of hydrogen devoured in seconds by an immense burst of flame, directly above the large, empty airfield in New Jersey where it was trying to land, less than a hundred miles from Edgar's home! The construction of a backyard igloo by the gang of kids after the big snowfall! The woman hit by a Chevrolet who lands, dead as a doornail, on the school playground!

And then, toward the end, you can delight in the description of the World's Fair's pavilions and the people who ambled around them, open-mouthed, perennially astonished, admiring and grateful for the opportunity to feel themselves part of what they believed would come soon, in the impending future. And in the closing pages, when Edgar's parents are deeply moved to read in the *New York Times* that their son's essay has won a runner-up prize in a children's essay contest sponsored by the World's Fair, you will be able to be as deeply moved as they were, and as I was.

I decide that I need to tell Ettore all about it immediately, the story of the 1939 World's Fair, in part because we're almost home by now, and I start to talk, but I get worked up, and I start to summarize, and when you summarize it's always a form of betrayal, a graceless process of omission, so I get overheated and stumble over my words and before I know it, instead of science, I find myself talking to him about science fiction and myself as a boy, and at a certain point I say the following words to him, *That savage spirit of innovation and change that sprang out of the roots of science fiction and invaded the world, keeping boys and girls up at night as they fantasized about what a wonderful life they'd live, with the endless procession of new technological products.*

He turns around and stares at me, surprised at my emphasis, and so I tell him that once I saw it myself, only once, in 1984, during the opening ceremonies of the Los Angeles Olympics, when that little man in the jet pack zoomed back and forth over the Memorial Coliseum, leaving the whole world slackjawed in amazement.

"So, basically, the Jetsons," Ettore replies, with a smile.

"The who?"

"The Jetsons, those cartoons Angelica and I used to watch on TV when we were little, don't you remember?"

"Well, actually, no, I don't..."

"Oh, yeah, definitely. The Jetsons were the science fiction version of the Flintstones...They went everywhere in jet packs and spaceships, and they had robots to do their housecleaning and they had holograms...The Jetsons, Babbo, come on, I can't believe you never saw them...Oh, look, we're home. Can I borrow the car tonight? Do you mind?"

If Gordon's Right

I might have to blame the Riesling that I drank at dinner to celebrate the return of my young son, but now that I'm alone in the backyard and Carlotta has gone to sleep, and I don't feel like sleeping, I continue to think about the terrible sentences that Gordon writes to maintain that the Special Century was a singular event, with a beginning and an end, a unique and never-to-be-repeated accident of History, because so many of its stunning conquests could only, by their very nature, happen once, since it's impossible to invent or discover electricity and the telephone and penicillin and the internal combustion engine a second time, and I have to admit that, if he's right, we're looking at a very serious problem.

If Gordon is right, then that means we're no longer capable of creating even one more of those Great Inventions that suddenly make whatever came before them obsolete and force the world to bend toward the new, as when long-distance airlines came into the world and people stopped using ocean liners to cross the oceans.

If it's true that the development brought by technological progress has substantially ground to a halt, because for more than a hundred years now we've been doing nothing more than improving our grandparents' Great Inventions and now we've come to their furthest limitations, then it does in fact mean that we're living in the deeply decrepit and decadent world that Carpini raved on about, and moreover it would mean that not only have the great overarching nineteenth-century ideas our civilization is still based on reached their maximum possible point of development, but also perhaps that our very civilization has finally reached the end of the line.

Because the "advances since 1970 have tended to be channeled into a narrow sphere of human activity having to do with entertainment, communications, and the collection and processing of information," as Gordon put it when discussing the growth that has sprung from the so-called digital revolution, and which won't be sufficient—*can't* be sufficient—to transport seven billion people through the twenty-first century and ensure them a decent livelihood, *otherwise they already would have done so.*

Not even the most enthusiastic of all techno-optimists can still fall for the laughable notion that the jobs lost to globalization can be replaced by jobs created with the digital revolution. Not when we're faced with millions of unemployed men and women, in Europe and in America, people who spend their days messaging each other and watching videos and posting pictures of dogs and cats and sunsets, overjoyed that they can buy at any hour of the day and night junk they can't use and useless services with the miserable pittance of their welfare checks, while they waste their lives and their eyesight—no, while we waste *our* lives and *our* eyesight—reading the messages of hatred that ooze out of the social networks, believing that they're real, believing that they're written by men and woman rightly infuriated at the state of the Western world, when in point of fact, those messages, insulting and denigrating and lying and sowing quarrels, are sent by none other than bots, programs created to undermine and destabilize and ultimately control our precarious and wobbling system by dictatorships that want only to watch that system collapse so that they can take advantage of it. Empires without liberty and without democracy that have appropriated the digital revolution that we have created, by means of that very same liberty and democracy, and then they've turned that revolution against us. Because by now it ought to be completely evident to even the stupidest observers that with all those billions of messages of hatred, Russia and China are quite simply waging war against us in the most intelligent and contemporary way imaginable.

At the end of his review of *The Rise and Fall of American Growth*, Krugman points out that, of course, Gordon could be wrong, and that it might just be a matter of time, a few years or so, before something else comes along to revolutionize our lives, changing them for the better: from the fields of biology, genetics, or artificial intelligence.

Who knows if that's true, or if it's possible.

Who knows if we'll have the good luck to live in another Special Century.

Because, if Gordon is right, the age that's just ended—that twentieth century, filled with wars and slaughter and hatred and grief and racism, but also rights and freedoms achieved and won, supreme heights of art, music, film, and literature—was actually the Golden Age, and we might not see anything like it again for centuries or perhaps, even, ever.

If Gordon is right, it means that there's been a huge party in this world that lasted for a century, and only Western people were invited to this party. And not even all of the Western peoples—that is, if it even means anything to call ourselves Westerners anymore, or if it ever did—but in any case, that millions and millions of people lived for decades with the constant spectacle of technological progress turning into economic growth before their eyes, penetrating their lives and filling them with hopes and ambitions and dreams of prosperity, taking them all the way up to the surface of the moon.

If Gordon is right, and it turns out that the party ended more or less at that very moment, while Armstrong danced awkwardly and gloriously in the Sea of Tranquility, then it means that what has ended, along with the Special Century, is the West itself, the West that we knew, where we were born, and with it, the absurd and thrilling idea of endless progress and endless growth and full employment that it brought with it, and it's pointless for us to knock ourselves out searching for it. Otherwise we'll wind up just like the guy who used to show up every Saturday night outside the locked gate of Gatsby's house, because no one had told him that Gatsby was dead, and that there weren't going to be any more parties.

If Gordon is right, all that we can do now, we who showed up late and only got to witness the last hurrahs of the big party, is to stave off the worst damage—because any party where the guests had a genuinely good time always leaves behind it a heap of garbage, all the filth that's necessary for any self-respecting binge—and grab brooms and mops and clean up and then hand over the world to our daughters and sons, who already seem to have figured out that they're bound to see very few parties in their time on this earth, and who have an overwhelming desire, and every right of their own, to take the reins of this place from day one.

We were robbed of our future, you lied to us and you gave us false hope.

Ah, maybe we should just get out of the way—we who are older than forty!

I clutch in my hand the glass with the last slurp of Riesling—I like my Riesling *trocken*, or dry, and ice-cold: I know that connoisseurs shudder at the idea of wines served excessively chilled, but I know what I like, and those connoisseurs are welcome to drink all the lukewarm wine that they please—and I get to my feet as I start to hear the rising notes of the distant music from the discotheques along the waterfront. It's their last hurrah, because in just a few days their closure orders will be taking effect, and I think about how many young men and women are bound to infect each other tonight, perhaps even Ettore and Angelica, who are down there with their friends and companions. I tell myself that I can't do anything but hope that the worst doesn't happen—that that's just what fathers and mothers do when their children grow up and leave home: they fear the world they had no misgivings about when they were young, when they were just dying to get out into that world and test themselves against it. Instead now they sit up worrying, helplessly, late into the night, resigning themselves to the understanding that their sons and daughters, when all is said and done, will share the fates of their contemporaries, just as we did with ours.

And then I realize that these thoughts—all the thoughts I've had this evening—are probably my first thoughts as an old man, and I'm tempted to laugh, and then I raise the glass with my last sip of Riesling to dedicate it to Babbo, as if uttering his name in this silent pine grove, but then I decide that I'd better not, and I switch off my brain and head off to bed.

September Arrives

This year at Forte dei Marmi the Feast of St. Hermes (Sant'Ermete) isn't being celebrated. On account of the virus, no market, no bonfire (*focone*) in the main piazza, no fireworks from the dock, so I might as well head back to Prato, because it's practically September now anyway, the month that ought theoretically to be the moment of the *redde rationem* in the Gospel, the time to give an accounting of your actions, perhaps even the eve of Armageddon.

The streets and roads are filled with a twitching, angry flow of traffic. Everyone's driving too fast. The mood is turning ugly. I see people treat each other viciously, flipping each other off for failing to use their turn signals, arguing over parking spaces. Women especially, and that should come as no surprise, because the impact of the virus on families has hit them hardest, and the imminent reopening of the schools is going to weigh unfairly on them. *Everything* seems to aim at and weigh unfairly on them.

I'm uneasy too. I never manage to relax. The television, the newspapers, the conversations of people I chance to overhear in the street, even the sky and the clouds all seem to conceal an impending *something*, the arrival of something terrible, as if the time we were living in had never been anything but a loan.

The infections are multiplying day by day, not only in Italy but all across Europe, and by now it's clear that, as the chorus of TV experts has begun to say, we're going to have to learn to live with the virus, which means hoping that only a very few get seriously ill. Because if the hospitalizations and ICU cases rise sharply in number, then we'll all be locked down at home again—there's no likelihood of our government going back on its word—and the same thing will happen more or less everywhere, in countries around the world, roughly simultaneously, because we're all connected, all migrants in this life, huddled together in the same immense boat to which globalization has relegated us.

Luciano Cimmino tells me that he's rather frightened, because hundreds of positive young men and women have returned to Naples from Capri and Sardinia—so strange to have to write this nowadays; strange and painful to see how the expression "being positive," should have now taken on a negative, *extremely* negative meaning—and are spreading the virus all over the city.

When I tell him that the situation seems to be under control, though, seeing that hospitalizations aren't rising, he tells me that it's impossible to know what's going to happen. That we're living in a situation of total uncertainty, in our lives and in our work.

"We're working on a high wire, hanging in a void, Edoardo, dangling from a thread that could snap at any second. If the situation got any worse and they had to order another lockdown, it would be an utter disaster."

Elisa tells me that she doesn't really know whether they sell the wine or not. She just makes it, and that's that. They're harvesting the grapes, but in some parts of the countryside, hail has devastated the vineyards, as if they needed some new disaster to add to the mix.

"This has been a strange season, anyway. For the grapes, as well as everything else. They're ripening early in some areas and very late in others. Grapes that look as if they've been boiled and other grapes that just never seem to ripen at all; grapes with low pH readings, which means they're very good, acceptable levels of acidity, and grapes with levels of acidity that have plummeted close to zero...Anyway, we're getting used to this kind of thing, these are years when there's not one harvest that's anything like the year before..."

The Mage says that nothing's moving in the textiles sector, and that's the way it is just about everywhere, in all the markets. Even at Zara, they're just waiting to understand what's going to happen next with this spike in infections. He was in Paris, and his clients were telling him that the summer-wear sales had gone reasonably well, but now he can't say what'll happen next. He's started traveling again; today he's in Milan. He gets around, the Mage does. He makes sure he shows his face. He talks to everyone. And everyone tells him the same thing. That no one knows anything. And that things are tough.

"I was on Corso Como the other night: completely deserted. A woman who runs a clothing store told me that three thousand people who usually work in the Towers nearby are at home now, doing what they call smart working...It's a mess, Edoardo, and not just for the textile industry."

"What about in America? What do you hear from our friend Donati?"

"Our friend Donati has just gone back to New York, and there too, nothing is moving. It's a city of ghosts, he says. There's nobody out and about. All the restaurants are shut, and so are the hotels. It's unrecognizable, nothing like the place we knew and loved. There too, everyone is working from home, all the shops are closed. No tourists whatsoever, because basically you can't even go to America anymore if you don't have a green card, and there are practically no flights now. The economy is in worse shape there than here in Italy..."

"What about La Torre? What is your company going to do?"

"I don't know, but the general mood is terrible, Edo. And the mass media isn't helping. The TV news is talking about nothing but the virus, all they report on is the number of infections and dead...How many people die of heart attacks every day, huh? It's not like that in Paris, you know. I mean, they're talking about Covid, but not to the exclusion of everything else. Here it's all anyone talks about…"

Alberto Galassi, from the Ferretti Group, calls me. They build yachts, the legendary Riva motorboats. He read an interview I did and wants to extend his compliments: "I really liked what you said about your grandmother, that she went to school as a girl in a horse-drawn gig, and then over the course of her life, she saw the Americans land on the moon, and she drove around in your father's eight-cylinder Mercedes… How are you doing?"

"Oh, well, I'm all right, I guess. How about you? How's work?"

"Excellent. July 2020 was better than July 2019. We're privileged, of course, but we're doing well… The lockdown's been hard on us, like it has on everybody, but we started up again, going great guns. The fifteen hundred people who work for us aren't worried, because they know that we've adopted the strictest anti-Covid security protocols, and that we're a healthy, debt-free company…"

"You sell the world's most beautiful boats to the world's richest people…"

"They're not boats, Edoardo. We sell 'private islands,' whether they're thirty feet long or three hundred feet long. Do you know that we make a solid-steel yacht that's 230 feet long? It's gorgeous, a real spectacle, I'll send you a video..."

"What do you expect from this fall?"

"As Forrest Gump used to say, life is like a box of chocolates, you never know what you're gonna get. Anyway, I'm super optimistic, in spite of the fact that this government hasn't done a thing for the factory workers and craftsmen, choosing instead to look out for the state bureaucrats and everyone with the 'citizen's income,' or guaranteed minimum income."

"Well, so how do you see it?"

"Let me ask you a question. In any catastrophic event, there are four phases: war, postwar, reconstruction, recovery. Which phase do you think we're in? You tell me... There's no vision of things... We're like World War One biplane pilots, flying blind through the clouds, able to see only the nose of their plane... And let me say it again, I'm a privileged individual talking to you, I sell private islands and I have the best nautical brands in the world... If I stop to think what it must be like in other sectors, I feel like crying..."

"So what do you expect? What's going to happen?"

"My group will continue to sell strongly, but Italy...I don't know, there are times when I'm filled with nostalgia, when I miss the world we grew up in, even though we were surrounded by terrorism and attacks and kidnappings, and our classmates were shooting up heroin, and yet we had the strength of mind to react, and we had this enormous spirit, such energy and determination, a real sense of momentum...We experienced true freedom, and we weren't afraid of anything, because we knew that we'd do all right in any case...Forgive me for the free-associating, I'll stop bothering you with my ramblings, ciao."

He hangs up, and thirty seconds later he sends me a video via WhatsApp in which a famous actor is sailing through Venice by night aboard a gleaming, magnificent Riva boat. He gives a book to a little boy while the theme music to Fellini's *8½* strikes up and a voice in the background repeats, *Never stop dreaming*.

I call Livia Firth, a cofounder of Eco-Age, a consulting and creative agency that communicates and teaches ethical sustainability to international brands. She is a tireless crusader for a new kind of fashion that's diametrically opposed to fast fashion.

"Livia, what's going to happen?"

"Lots of wonderful things. Yesterday, someone tried to give me a rubber eraser with *Erase 2020* written on it, but I refused to take it. I don't want to erase any part of 2020. That's where the change is going to begin. No, better, that's where the rebirth is going to begin."

"You're an optimist…"

"Very much an optimist. We've entered a new era, and nothing is ever going to be the same. Covid was a terrible shock, and it's not over yet, but change grows out of shocks. It needs shocks. We're going to have to rebuild everything…A world, a civilization, the way we think…But we're going to have to start from people, from values. From a sense of community, of belonging to the same planet…"

"The economy is on its knees…"

"It'll get up and back on its feet if everything changes. Strategies, objectives, ways of measuring economic performance. Companies need to change, and right away. *Sustainable* is more than just a cunning buzzword to use on journalists. It's an enormous and demanding commitment. But it's necessary. And day after day, consumers are placing more value on it. Because it has value. Because it's a foundational value to start out from, in fact, it is *the* foundational value."

"What about everyone who's seen their jobs vanish into thin air? The ones who are struggling right now? What do we say to them?"

"But it's not like the world was going all that well before Covid. The world wasn't in balance. No, the world was a disaster, Edoardo. Billions of people were starving, or else they were working all day for a handful of rice. Whole populations lacked clean water to wash with. Children were dying of diseases that could be cured for a few euros. And yet nobody was doing anything about it. Nothing ever changed. Everyone just stood around clapping for Greta, and then it was off at a gallop to H&M to buy some fast-fashion glad rags. We need to start taking care of people. Of everyone. I know that so many are going to suffer. *But so many more have been suffering as long as time itself.* And for that matter, if an apartment building collapses, what do you do? Do you stand there in front of the smoking ruins, or do you build a new and better one to replace it?"

I ask my butcher, Rino Pratesi, how his work has been going during the lockdown.

"Listen, Edoardo, I'm just starting to catch my breath now. During the quarantine my sales were up 40 percent. I had to call my brother to come in and help me because I couldn't keep up on my own."

"How come?"

"Maybe because people were afraid to go to the supermarket, or maybe they just didn't want to stand in line for an hour…Who knows why…But they all came and shopped here, they bought from me…"

"And now, Rino?"

"Now I'm still doing great."

"Better than last year?"

"Better than last year."

The phone rings. It's my brother Lorenzo, who's a day trader who works from his living room. He tells me that at the European Central Bank no one has any idea of the problems facing labor and they need to hurry up and get money out to people.

"But not to the banks. To the people, directly, to their bank accounts. They need to immediately institute a guaranteed income to all citizens of the European Union! But there's something else I want to ask you…The stock exchanges are all going strong, they're skyrocketing, and I'm happy about that, but I'm not sure I understand exactly why. What does Guido have to say?"

FAANG Stocks

Guido would be Guido Brera, the financier, the manager of large fortunes extraordinaire, the author of novels and television series. He also happens to be married to Caterina Balivo, the presenter and actress.

"What's going to happen, Guido?"

"I don't know. No one knows. If you leave aside the whole online sector of the economy, nothing else is moving."

"The government has already budgeted nearly a hundred billion and no one seems to be going back to work…"

"What else could they do? I understand them. The only response they knew how to offer was monetary, and that's what they did. Like all the other govern-ments, for that matter. The deficits were exploding, the GDPs were collapsing, and so they set about printing money to try to keep an engine running that would have otherwise coughed and shuddered to a halt. But it's an engine that's already barely turning over, a transmission that has no real grip on its tires."

"Then why have the stock markets risen so sharply? It makes no sense, give me a break. The economy is on its knees, people are out of jobs around the world, and the stock exchanges are all going crazy. What's going on?"

"By now it's carved in stone, irrevocably, that interest rates are going to remain at zero for a long time, and the more money you create, the more that money loses its intrinsic value. You create a form of inflation that's not demand-driven, the kind that comes from consumer spending...It's another kind of inflation, very different. And far worse. It's asset-driven inflation..."

"It's what?"

"All this money that's being created has to go *some-where*, and if the return on bonds is zero, then inves-tors are going to look for bigger yields elsewhere. In real assets. The first place to put the cash is in stocks."

"But companies are doing terribly…"

"No, Edoardo, *certain companies* are doing terribly. Everything that's digital is going great guns, and has been doing even better than during Covid. I said so in March, when everything was collapsing, that it was time to invest in the markets. But it hardly took a genius to figure it out, all you needed was a dose of sangfroid, of cold-blooded nerve. Trillions—*trillions*—of dollars and euros were being printed, and where do you think that money was going? Stay calm, keep your eyes open, and you'll see that Facebook, Amazon, Apple, Netflix, and Google, the FAANG stocks, are continuing to do well, and you buy them."

"But hadn't their stock prices already risen plenty?"

"They'll just go on climbing."

"But why?"

"Because we've entered a future where these companies are going to count more and more, not less. They're going to earn more, not less. They've conquered the world. Put together, they're worth almost seven trillion dollars. They're worth as much as countries, and they talk directly to countries, as peers, as equals. They're incredibly powerful companies, entirely digital, and the virus only helps them. FAANG stocks are going to become the world's strongest currency, they'll take the place of the dollar, wait and see..."

"That seems impossible to me..."

"No, no, it's all perfectly rational. Easy to explain. It's a world that's changing, and that world doesn't care what anyone thinks. Just think about office work...We handed over our factories to the Chinese and held on to our offices, and now office work has become obsolete and is vanishing, replaced by working from home. It's going to be an immense revolution. We're going to have to rethink our big cities. London, New York, Chicago, Milan, Shanghai, and Beijing lived off office space, and now the offices are empty, and they're not going to fill up again anytime soon. Smart working is here to stay. Companies have discovered that there's no reason to spend money on rent and expenses and transportation and travel and conferences and conventions and bonuses...They just keep everyone at home, and they're available whenever needed by Zoom. They'll save millions and exploit their workers more thoroughly."

"What about secondary economic sectors?"

"That's another major problem: shops, restaurants, cafés, and gymnasiums. Delivery people, bartenders, baristas, and waiters, they're all doing work that requires no special credentials, and their jobs are going to disappear. It's been calculated that for every white-collar worker who stops going to the office, five people less qualified than he or she is will lose their jobs..."

"And then what will happen?"

"We're going to have to institutionalize a universal income. We'd have had to do it anyway, but the pandemic just accelerated the process. We're going to have to brace for millions of jobless around the world. For that matter, a society based on technology can't be inclusive, nobody believes that anymore. Everyone who's excluded from that society, and they are millions of people, is going to have to be helped. But they can't be sent to work in factories, because here in Europe we're producing less and less, and so the forms of social welfare are going to have to become structural. Government budgets are going to have to set aside an ever-growing share for individual subsidies. Either that, or face growing social tensions."

"And what's going to happen to Italy?"

"I don't foresee any major collapses. No revolts, no apocalyptic disasters. We're not going to wind up like

Piranesi's shepherds, grazing our sheep at the foot of the ruins of an empire. There's going to be a slow decline, a long gentle downward slide, but nothing traumatic. Remember that in this country the tragedies always happen offstage. And then money will arrive from Europe...Neither Germany nor France will let us go the way of Greece. Italy is a market of highly evolved consumers, after all. Who would they sell their cars and handbags and lipsticks to, without us?"

"So what does that mean?"

"It means that one way or another we're going to be given money to buy what other people are producing."

"What about the public debt?"

"We can't worry about the public debt right now. Not during a pandemic."

I remain silent for a good long while.

"Edo, are you still there?"

"Sure, I'm here. I was just thinking about that thing Guicciardini said, do you remember it? *De' futuri contingenti non v'è scienza* (About the unknowns of the future we cannot guess)."

"Yes, of course."

"Well, in the past few months I've talked to lots and lots of people, and I've asked them all about

the future...What's going to happen next, how are
we going to handle things...And all of them, of
course, have replied that they had no idea what's
going to happen, because nobody knows that, but
then they launch right in, each making their own
sets of predictions...Because it's only human, I
would guess...No one can resist the temptation of
trying to predict the future, and that's always been
the case, just think of the oracles, the augurs and
sibyls, or astrology and its horoscopes...But it's
different for you. The very work you do is a daily
act of defiance against what Guicciardini has to
say. Every single day you go out and bet, if that's
the right word, on what's going to happen in the
future. And you stake large amounts of money on
these bets of yours...Billions of euros of your clients' money...And often, if not always, you hit the
nail on the head...So what does that mean? Does
it mean that Guicciardini was wrong and *De' futuri
contingenti* v'è *scienza*? (About the unknowns of
the future we *can* guess?) Is it possible to predict
the future? And if so, how?"

I hear him sigh.

"I don't know, I'd never thought of it in these
terms. I carry out a constant process of reading

events, because for the work I do, I have to be familiar with both the present and the past...Finance, the history of finance, certainly, but also literature, also poetry...Because the future has its curves, it's not carved in stone...There are interactions of forces, and they determine the future...I don't know if that makes sense to you...It's a sort of dance, the markets dance...But then singularities, anomalies come along, like this virus, and the future is rewritten...There are tempests...as the poet Alda Merini put it, *I did not know that to be born deranged, to open clumps of dirt, could unleash storms*...The market is a vicious beast, it always delights in the game of making you look like a fool, and you need to know how to bend to its whims, and think, watch, focus, hit hard when necessary, sometimes very hard indeed, firing all the artillery at your disposal..."

To hear him talk so thoughtfully about dance, about Alda Merini, and the cannonballs, I'm reminded of when Sergio Vari told the technicians at the woolen mill and me that certain new samples were no good—"They have no light, they need more light"—and as we all gazed at him, baffled, asking him if he meant they should be a lighter shade, he went over to the window and pointed up at the sky, saying, "You see the sky? There, that's the light we ought to be seeing in these samples..."

"It's like a poison circulating in your body, an obsession, a pain," Guido continues. "Managing money is managing pain, because any decision you make, you're a part of it, there's all of you in it, your convictions, your vision of the world, your sleepless nights...And you have to have the moral strength to maintain your position when it all goes wrong, because not everything happens when you want it to...And so you have doubts, you suppose that you've made a mistake, and every day that goes by, you lose a mountain of cash, and you stop sleeping, you suffer like a dog because the obsessive persistence in finding confirmation for your beliefs never leaves you, and you're certain that you're right, and yet the stock price still drops, or rises, and the whole time you're losing your clients' money...It is a genuine source of pain, because changing your mind hurts, but sometimes you have to do it. To say *I was wrong*, reset everything, and start over without thinking about it again. Never fall in love with your own ideas, never. Only fall in love with your significant other. And then, Edo, when the pain becomes too much, you have to stop."

It's Evening

I t's evening, and from the terrace of my home I watch the sun illuminate the sky with golden light, like in some canvas by Ed Ruscha, as it drops down toward the horizon, toward the blessed Versilia, where my wife and children have gone for the last weekend of summer, and where I'll go too, tomorrow morning.

Beneath me, there stretches out a panorama of industrial sheds, by and large reconverted: their proud asbestos roofs transmuted into expanses of solar panels, the fiercely ostentatious signs bearing the owner's surname replaced by the garish neon colors of the signs of mini-markets, Chinese discount houses, and car washes.

One after another they fill the eye and march on to the hills of Montalbano, barely contained behind the straight lines of the roads and the last scattered fields, left untilled and untended. I know them all, down to the very last one of them. They're rough and ungainly, and for decades they've been the shelters and the temples of that poor and sentimental economy that every day whispers its aching, sorrowful story to me.

Soon, in the darkness, all that will disappear. Hundreds of lights will flick on, and the plain that runs from Florence to Pistoia—in the Pleistocene epoch it was a single immense lake, and the first one to realize that was Leonardo da Vinci—is going to turn into a replica of Los Angeles.

I drink the first, icy sip of the gin and tonic I prepared for myself in careful accordance with the unchanging liturgy I've always followed. I filled my glass with ice, I dropped in a slice of one of those oversize lemons from Campania, I poured over it all the exact right dollop of an exceedingly dry gin made nearby, in the tiny town of Tavola, so close that I can see it from my house—Tavola, a subdivision of Prato, about which Malaparte wrote in *Maledetti toscani* (Those cursed Tuscans), *But try to find that renowned Tuscan gentility at Campi Bisenzio, or at Prato, Tavola, Jolo, Pisa, Arezzo, Empoli, Figline, or just across the Arno at San Frediano*—and then I added the tonic water, which absolutely must be good old Schweppes tonic water, and not one of these new and fancy varieties, after which I mixed it, not long and not vigorously, because you don't want to lose the fizz, because I like my gin and tonic light and dry, chilled, bubbly, and scented with lemon.

I sense my father close to me.

My father, who's no longer among us, my childhood and lifelong idol, my basic point of reference, my example and my ultimate goal, a thousand times better than all the fathers in books and movies, the everyday hero with a spectacular name, a name better suited to the protagonist of an adventure novel than to him, who'd always declared his pride in being a member of the bourgeoisie: Alvarado Gualberto.

There were never any epic triumphs or disastrous collapses in his life. No fortunes earned or lost, no heartbreaking love stories, no illegitimate children scattered across the face of the globe. No murders, thefts, narcotics, shoot-outs, hatreds, vendettas, bankruptcies, trials, mysterious and incurable diseases, no time behind bars. There was the war, true, but it was only seen from a distance, as a childhood memory. No politics, never politics, and almost no religion to speak of, save for perhaps late in life, in his final years, and he experienced that in his own personal fashion too.

His was not an adventurous life, unless you choose to consider running a business an adventure. If you chose to summarize that life with the chilly brusqueness of those Anglo-Saxon epitaphs that amused him so deeply, we might say that it went more or less as follows: born in Prato, he studied briefly, went to work as a young man, married, had three children and made some money, and at age eighty-five he left this world.

Every so often I go to visit him in the cemetery, and when I come face-to-face with the little plaque featuring a photograph of his cheerfully smiling face from some party back in the seventies, with a mustache and hair allowed to grow slightly overlong, well, some sort of self-defense or rescue system snaps into operation inside me, I can't quite describe it, but it just cuts all the wires and turns me into an automaton that feels nothing and experiences nothing.

I spend a few minutes there, without a thought in my head, looking at his photograph and the swooping flourishes of his name, in the typeface chosen by my brother, and then I turn to go, disappointed at this haphazard visit, but as soon as I reach the steps, before I've walked more than fifty feet or so, I turn around and come back, because I can't believe that I've been there long enough. Maybe I just need to spend more time there—every single time the same ineffectual thoughts—and I stand there, facing the plaque and I look at the picture and the same system snaps into operation and once again I feel absolutely nothing.

Every time, *every single time*, it's the same thing.

I've found myself doing the same thing as many as three times in a row, this to-and-fro among the headstones and the stairs, which really is basically insane, and it's a good thing that no one can see me—it seems to me that people just don't visit cemeteries the way they used to, because every time I go to see my babbo I walk down two long corridors lined with small vaults, and I'm always alone—until, at a certain juncture, my brain just shuts down, and that's the end of the day.

That's what's just happened.

Half an hour ago.

Because by now the infections are spreading like wildfire throughout Europe, and we're already hearing talk of shutting down cafés and restaurants, and since the next logical step, or maybe even the step previous to the dining and drinking establishments, would be shutting down the cemeteries, I'd decided to go and visit him. It probably won't amount to much, having stood there for a while in front of his plaque, empty-headed, but it's certainly worth *something*, and maybe, one day, I'll figure out exactly *what*.

My memories of him burn like shattered fragments of the fuselage of an airplane that's just plowed into the earth, the sole scorching fragmented remains of the flight of a great airliner, suddenly cut short.

He didn't much care for the past, and he never wanted to talk to me about it, especially not his own personal past—*What are you doing, digging down into what's done and over, you knucklehead? Life is now, and even more so, it's tomorrow*—which is gone now, because the people who knew him best back in the old days—his three sisters, Alba, Loredana, and Aldiana; and Ardengo, Pedra, Giuliano, and

Alfiero—are all dead just like he is, and when they died they took their poor and exaggeratedly, pointlessly highfalutin names with them.

He was born in 1932, on April 6, in Narnali, an outlying subdivision of Prato, in a tiny little two-story row house, with a tiny backyard garden and a minuscule truck garden, lined up alongside dozens of other houses just like it on the Via Pistoiese, just before the Viaccia bridge.

His mother was named Rosa, and she was a big strapping woman with a constant smile, and she'd always tell me that I had white teeth. She died when I was still just a child, thirteen years after the death of her husband Temistocle, my grandfather, whose name I bear. He died young, before I was born, and was a grim and moody and taciturn man who refused to accept high-handed treatment from others, and who had never worked for anybody but himself, and who spent the whole week at his loom, until lunchtime on Sunday, whereupon he'd climb onto his motorcycle and roar off to Pistoia, to his whores.

I know almost nothing about my father's childhood. I don't know where he went to school, whether he liked it or not, whether he was a good student or not. I don't know what he did, what he thought, what he liked or didn't like, how he dressed or how he wore his hair.

I can only rely on what little he'd told me.

Pictures, mostly.

The retreating Germans who blew up the large factory room with the three slow, titanic looms owned by Temistocle and his brother Omero, the embryo of the future factory to come, and the whole time those German soldiers had had their machine guns leveled at the people of Narnali, assembled and forced to watch, and my father with them, watching, trembling all over, holding *his* father's hand, my grandfather's hand.

The American troops parading festively through Prato in their jeeps just days later, giving him a chocolate bar, packs of chewing gum and cigarettes.

The murder of a Fascist on the Piazza delle Carceri, in Prato, and the blood spouting out of his head after a partisan shot him at point-blank range.

The Gerosa 125, his first and only motorcycle, which he rode to Florence when he was eighteen, in the rain or the wind, to learn English and German at the Berlitz school.

And that's all.

My father's past is something that needs to be darned and mended and stitched back together, like the tattered cloth of his frank and open and hard-working life, inseparable from his work and the fervid years in which that life was lived to the hilt, because my father was a product of his time, and like millions of other Italians, he'd felt the thrill of ambition surging through him. He'd found it to be a good and just thing, and for decades he had kept his head down and worked hard to attain and preserve an economic prosperity that, however, he never allowed to take over his life, a life that grew animated and ennobled primarily the moment he stepped foot outside the factory, and then indeed his life grew rich and intensely private, when there was no more room for work—I never heard him talk about business, outside of the woolen mill—and he could enjoy himself as he lived his life just as he pleased, at last.

How, at age thirty, free as a bird because he wouldn't meet and immediately marry my mother until a full year later, he decided to go up to Sankt Moritz—Saint Moritz—to celebrate the end of the year.

The year was 1962, and he'd agreed to travel from Prato with three friends, but the day before the scheduled departure the other three pulled out, and he decided to go anyway, on his own. He climbed into his green Fiat 1500, went to Milan, and from there he took the bus to Sankt Moritz, because back then there was a direct connection.

Once there, he'd checked into a pension, but he went to the big New Year's party at the Palace Hotel, the finest hotel in Sankt Moritz, and he wore the tuxedo he'd brought with him from Prato, all gleaming and black.

He didn't know anyone, of course, but he cut a fine figure, my babbo did, and it didn't take him long to make the acquaintance of a gorgeous young woman, *a sort of double for Claudia Cardinale*, and as he was dancing with her he seemed to notice that, pirouetting around him, fitting snugly into his perfect tuxedo and arm in arm with a lady who appeared to be his wife and who was as short and stout and dumpy as he was, was none other than one of his personal idols. So when the song came to an end, my father went over to him and asked him, "Are you Alfred Hitchcock?"

And Hitchcock, imperturbably, replied: "Yes, I am."

And then they bade each other farewell and each went to his own table, and Babbo said nothing more to him because this Hitchcock had struck him as someone who was *full of himself.*

Or the time that Ella Fitzgerald came to Prato, to the Teatro Metastasio, and when the concert was over, she leaned out toward the audience, which was caught up in a delirium of joy, pressing up against the stage, and everyone was reaching up to grip her hand except Babbo, who thought it hardly seemed elegant to shake hands with a goddess. So he climbed up onto the stage and ceremoniously kissed her hand, to a deluge of fervent applause, in what, as far as I am able to tell, was his one and only public act.

This is all I can remember about him, this and nothing else.

The wonderful things, the antics.

Like the time, at age sixty, that he stubbornly decided to get his certification as a scuba diver and went to Sharm El-Sheikh, Egypt, for a week with all the divers from his class, going into the water with tanks on his back, morning and afternoon, all the way down to thirty meters.

He had always loved swimming, and he insisted on saying that his favorite stroke was the crawl—he never keep his head bobbing high above the water's surface like the lifeguards. In the placid sea off Forte dei Marmi he went on swimming until he was well over seventy, and I would stand there on the beach, my hand shielding my eyes to scan the sea, needlessly worried, trying to glimpse those strokes of his arms that I could recognize out of a thousand others—ample, slow, powerful—until I glimpsed him from a distance returning to shore, and then I'd follow him until he emerged from the water, drenched and dripping, and he seemed like Neptune, big and strong as he was, bigger than me, his muscles and chest swollen from the effort and his flesh striped from the jellyfish stings that he always used to say didn't bother him in the slightest.

I remember when, close to age seventy, he let his hair grow out so long that he had to tie it back in a ponytail, and the time he went to Botswana all by himself to see the lions, and found himself paddling a canoe in the Okavango Delta, surrounded by hippopotamuses the size of delivery vans, and even from out in the wilds of the savanna, he still managed to send long faxes to the factory, to be conveyed to my mamma, telling her how much he loved her.

And I remember the morning I told him that Bompiani was going to publish my novel, and he was speechless, until he found the words to congratulate me. But then, in the middle of the afternoon, he walked into my office with a very serious expression and asked how much money I'd paid Bompiani to have them publish my book, and I pretended to be indignant, but there was never a moment in my life when I loved him more.

This is what I can remember about him.

This, and only this, thank God.

The bad stuff is gone.

The grief and the horror remain out of the picture.

After selling the woolen mill—in 2004, when he was seventy-two—my father's life suddenly fell silent, and one day he called me to say that he felt like he was rolling forward *in neutral*.

He stayed more and more at home, immersed in long silences, during which, however, he never conveyed the idea that he was worried or unhappy or sad or disappointed or, as people say these days, "devoured by some demon." So we didn't worry about him, me or my siblings, in part because he always emerged happily from those silences, often in a fine mood, and he couldn't wait for lunchtime or dinnertime to roll around so he could eat plentifully and well, and drink a glass or two of those humble wines that he and he alone liked, and then he'd take out his cell phone and start sending us text message after text message, often tangled up and muddled because of his obstinate insistence on dictating those messages, and partly because of those humble wines.

Who can say what he glimpsed in the dozens of understated pictures of flowers and clouds and butterflies and sunsets, of my mother and my children, that he'd take, variously, with his phone or his old Nikon, and that he'd enlarge and print and leave scattered around the house, no longer of any interest to him.

Who can say what he heard in the symphonies of Beethoven and Mozart, just those two, and always the same ones, or the huge extemporaneous cacophonous din of the jazz he'd always loved and that now and then he'd shut himself up in his room and turn up the volume and listen to at full blast.

Who can say what he found in the newspapers—
one local paper and one national one—that every
morning, come hell or high water, he absolutely had
to go out to the newsstand and purchase and then
read from the front page to the back.

Sometimes I think that—like all the rest of us
who had worked in that factory for years and then,
one day, stopped—he just needed to continue to
drink at the watering trough of what had always
pleased him, as if he were in search of a confirmation that, while he might have lost the factory, he
hadn't lost Beethoven and Cole Porter and the Prato
edition of *La Nazione*, and he could still count on
these things to obtain crumbs of comfort—a happy
and worthy thought that could constitute the foundations on which to build his day, because when
you're living in neutral, you need to invent the way
to get to the end of each day, and that's not always
easy, or even possible, and any assistance is more
than welcome.

I believe that, like all of us—like me—he was
looking for another way of living in peace and tranquility, a sort of equilibrium, perhaps even a state
of serenity, so I never told him anything that could
possibly worry him or demand any answer other

than sure, okay, that was fine, absolutely outstanding, no problem.

He seemed to prefer things that way, in part because that's the way he acted with me, and we almost always found ourselves talking about trivial and insubstantial topics, and I continued to assure myself that it was better that way because, after all, if some truly serious issue arose, we'd have talked it over together the way we always did when he was still working in the plant. The only thing is that nothing important had been cropping up for some time now. With the troubles of age all that came his way were minor issues and bureaucratic headaches, the kind of stuff your CPA or your notary could take care of: taxes, road-use licenses, insurance policies, driver's license renewals, minor legal disagreements with neighbors, and the whole array of ball-busting annoyances that you can take in stride so easily when things are going well, but that bury you alive when you have nothing else to think about. And even if he never told me so, I knew that there were times he'd wake up at night and lie there in his bed, staring at the ceiling and worrying about all the terrible things that might happen to him if, to name one possibility, they refused to renew his license.

Now I can't say anymore whether it was good for him to call us up for years on end just to joke around like a teenager, and keep his other thoughts to himself, his black, vicious thoughts, the ones that really inflict pain.

I hope so, because the alternative is intolerable.

Everyone dreams about him, about my babbo.

My wife does.

My children do.

My siblings do.

My friends do.

The few relatives I have do. And so do my acquaintances.

And then they come to see me and tell me about their dream, which is more or less always the same.

He was smiling, they all say. *It was really him.*

He hugged me.

He was giving me a ride from Prato to Rome in his car, and your mamma kept asking me, "Who are you? Who are you?"

We were at the beach, the sun was shining, it was a beautiful day.

He was with your mamma, in the center of Prato.

He was doing just fine, in excellent shape.

He was diving into the sea, and then he started swimming until he vanished over the horizon, like that time he swam all the way around Panarea!

He looked like he was doing great.

He was smiling.

He was smiling.

He was smiling.

Cheerful, witty and sharp, the way he was.

Not me, though.

Since the morning he died, I still haven't dreamt about him.

Never, not even once.

He really loved America, and the first time he went, he took me and my mamma with him. It was 1976, the year of the bicentennial, and I was twelve.

After spending four days on our own in New York, we joined a guided tour that took us to seven cities in fifteen days. All we did was board and disembark from planes: we went to Buffalo to see Niagara Falls, to Washington, DC, to tour the White House, to New Orleans to watch jazz bands on Bourbon Street, to San Francisco to drive over the Golden Gate Bridge, to Las Vegas to gamble in the casinos and take a drive up and down the Strip in the immense white Cadillac Eldorado my father insisted on renting, and then, at last, we arrived in Los Angeles, where we took a bus tour of the homes of the movie stars and touched the water of the Pacific Ocean in Santa Monica, which we liked especially because of how much it reminded us of Forte dei Marmi.

In New York we stayed at the Waldorf Astoria, the legendary hotel that Babbo had chosen because he'd seen it so many times in the movies. On account of my jet lag, I was always awake super early, and I'd watch TV with the sound off to keep from waking them up, and as soon as the darkness started to fade I'd go over to the window, to watch the skyscrapers glowing in the dawn light, and I'd keep watching them until Babbo and Mamma woke up and we could go get a bacon-and-eggs breakfast and stroll up and down Park Avenue.

That's how our days in New York always began, with a bacon-and-eggs breakfast and a leisurely stroll up and down that big avenue, and while I'd get bored walking north, because there wasn't much to see besides the big apartment buildings and the well-to-do matrons walking their little lapdogs, followed by nannies pushing baby carriages, I really loved walking south down Park Avenue. I could keep my eyes glued on the Pan Am Building, because Babbo had told me that helicopters landed on the roof, and I promised myself that someday, when I was a grown-up, I too would arrive in Manhattan by helicopter.

My babbo and mamma seemed to be having the times of their lives on those walks. They peeked into the front lobbies of luxury apartment buildings and discussed with great animation which one they'd choose if they were forced, someday, to live there because they'd had to escape from Italy, and they always returned the greetings of the uniformed doormen who guarded the glass doors of those apartment buildings—the instant they saw the two of them coming, they would hasten to open the front door for them, thinking they were coming in to visit some resident of the building.

Because they were beautiful, my parents.

Beautiful as the noonday sun.

And they dressed nicely.

In New York, we also did all the things that tourists do. After all, it was the first time there for all three of us. The *cardati*—carded fabrics—made by our woolen mill, Lanificio T. O. Nesi & Figli, couldn't compete in that immense and largely unrefined market, price obsessed and stubbornly clinging to cottons and artificial fibers, and so this trip was a pure *pleasure trip*, as people used to say in the old days.

We took the ferry to see the Statue of Liberty, we rode up to the top of the Empire State Building and the Twin Towers, we strolled through Central Park, we visited the Metropolitan Museum in search of the Caravaggios—*Old Merisi!* Babbo would cry, filled with enthusiasm for everything. *Where is my old friend Merisi!*—the Museum of Modern Art to see Monet—*The water lilies!*—and Picasso—*Pablo! Pablo!*—and the department stores. We went to Tiffany's, too, and bought something for Mamma, I think it was a bracelet, and she was moved almost to tears.

The last day we spent in the city, Babbo decided to go to Coney Island, so we boarded the subway and rode all the way out there, dressed like proper citizens of Prato, Mamma with her daytime jewelry, Babbo with his Rolex, and me in my little dark blue Lacoste polo shirt.

Mamma kept looking around and saying under her breath that we'd made a mistake when we decided to take the subway, we should have taken a taxi, but Babbo just pointed around with a broad smile at the various passengers, Black and Puerto Rican and Chinese, crowding our subway car and told her that this was America, the melting pot, the Big Apple, and there was absolutely no reason to worry, and in fact, of course, no one bothered us, no one said a word to us, no one even gave us a second glance.

It took a long time to get there, and when we did it was a disappointment for me, Coney Island, because it turned out to be nothing more than a down-at-the-heels beachfront. Maybe it was because the attractions weren't running in the morning and the weather was cloudy, but it seemed to me like a drab, no-longer-fashionable place. But Babbo was in a great mood. He wouldn't stop telling us about all the scenes from movies that are set in Coney Island, and since the big Ferris wheel wasn't running, he insisted that I take a ride on a big iron-and-wood roller coaster that creaked and groaned and was terrifying just to look at from a distance, let alone ride on, and then he wanted to go down to the beach to touch the water of the Atlantic Ocean, and I went down with him and stuck my hand into that icy water.

For lunch we ate hot dogs purchased from one of those little carts, and then Mamma said that she'd had enough fun and wanted to head back to the hotel. Babbo tried to propose staying till nightfall to see the famous million electric light bulbs that all switched on at the same time, but she wouldn't be placated. I said nothing, because I was hoping she'd win the argument, and in fact she eventually had her way, so we all trooped back onto the subway to head back to Manhattan, still surrounded by menacing Blacks and Puerto Ricans who didn't give us so much as a first, much less a second glance.

When the hotel desk clerk greeted us on our return and asked what we had done that day and Babbo told him the whole story, everyone's eyes at the desk grew big and round and they told us that we'd been lucky, because it was very, *very* dangerous to take the subway to Coney Island.

Babbo was surprised, but Mamma flew into a rage, and there was even a brief spat. To get things back on track, we decided that we'd go to dinner at a first-rate restaurant, *the best place in the city, and Italian*, as Babbo decreed, stung to the quick, addressing the half-dozen uniformed porters who were garrisoning the reception desk at the Waldorf Astoria, well aware that they'd all made him look like a reckless fool in Mamma's eyes, and they made a reservation at Gino's, on Lexington Avenue.

I remember every detail perfectly. The walls were painted with black-and-white stripes at Gino's. Babbo took great pleasure in that fact, opining that the owners must be Juventus fans just like him. Then, as soon as we were seated, Mamma whispered that Frank Sinatra was sitting at the table right ahead of ours.

Babbo looked up from the menu and for a second looked at him, Sinatra, surrounded as he was by a retinue of good-looking, cheerful people, and then he smiled and said, *There he is, The Voice himself*, and when Mamma told him to go over, introduce himself, and shake hands with him, because he'd never get another opportunity like this one as long as he lived, he shook his head. When she went on pestering him, he proclaimed, *I have my personal dignity, Paola, and anyway, I LOVE JAZZ! The music I love passionately is jazz.* But at the end of the meal, when we got up from our table, Frank

Sinatra turned to look at Babbo and Mamma, because they really were as beautiful as the noonday sun, and then they exchanged a brief smile, my babbo and The Voice.

My finest memory, though, is of Los Angeles.

It was the last night of our stay there, and we were sitting at a small table at the bar that stood on the rooftop terrace of our hotel, just him and me, because Mamma was tired and had gone back to the room, and while we were looking out in companionable silence at the lights of that endless city that glittered, stretching out as far as the eye could see, he told me that, *as the grandson of a shoemaker and the son of a weaver,* he was proud that he'd actually been able to come and see America.

And then he told me that *the world was free and immense and filled with promises of happiness and prosperity,* and that if I doubled down, if I worked as hard as he had worked, it would go a hundred times better for me than it had for him, because instead of starting out from Narnali, I was starting out *from the world's rooftop.*

The sun has set, and the industrial sheds of Prato have become Los Angeles, their lights aglitter as far as the eye can see.

I turn around and I see him.

He's right next to me, sitting in his white easy chair, reading the newspaper.

I call to him and he turns around, sees me, and smiles.

Afterword

So much, so very much has happened since the day in November 2020 when *Sentimental Economy* was published in Italy, but there's no point in telling you about it here.

You know it, we all know it already.

Of the people you've just read about, two have already changed jobs. I'm glad to say that Giuseppe Conte is no longer the prime minister of Italy, while Enrico Giovannini has been appointed to the cabinet position of Minister of Sustainable Infrastructure and Mobility.

In spite of the disruptions to the global supply chain and the return of inflation, the economy—

sentimental or otherwise—surged powerfully in 2021, dispelling all fears and defying all predictions.

From the Malibu beach where he took refuge after finally managing to show his collection to his Los Angeles clients, the Mage phoned to tell me that he'd enjoyed a record year.

Elisa Martelli too had an excellent year, as did her red wines. And her Cabernet Franc was awarded the highly regarded Tre Bicchieri award.

Luciano Cimmino did much bigger business in 2021 than he did in 2019, before Covid even existed.

Livia Firth let me know that she had an excellent 2021, and she's already preparing for the imminent advent of the metaverse.

It was a record year for Alberto Galassi too. Millionaires are fighting to buy his boats—or should we say, his private islands—and his order book is full until 2023.

Rino Pratesi continues to sell his amazing roast beef.

And once again Guido Brera has emerged victorious from his duel with Guicciardini, successfully peering into the very same future about which he shouldn't by rights be able even to guess. His investments have gone spectacularly, especially his

FAANG stocks, and he has earned millions of euros for his clients.

"Then why do I feel so bad, Edo, why?" he writes me. "All of this suffering, all these deaths...All this anger...Tell me, why do I feel so bad?"

And I don't know what to tell him.

I feel bad myself.

These are strange days, as if medicated.

And to make things worse, we've lost Joan Didion.

Acknowledgments

I must thank Enrico Giovannini, Livia Firth, Alberto Magelli, Luciano Cimmino, Elisa Martelli, Rino Pratesi, Alberto Galassi, and Guido Brera for letting me interview them.

Serena Dandini, for having told me some time ago that what I wrote about was the *sentimental economy*.

And also Giovanni Veronesi, Valeria Solarino, Dario Di Vico, Teresa Ciabatti, Chiara Valerio, Carmine Schiavo, Mario Desiati, Sandro Veronesi, Valerio Barberis, Roberto Santini, Francesco Meli, Cosimo Pacciani, Mario Paloschi, and Salvatore Federico.

Ugo Marchetti, fundamental and irreplaceable.

My siblings.

Elisabetta, Eugenio, and the whole Nave di Teseo.

Carlotta, Angelica, and Ettore.